Building Trans
Kindness in Schools

Being kind in education is about much more than being nice. This unique book shows how transformational kindness needs to be an explicit, essential part of classroom and school culture in order to improve student success.

Author Hope E. Wilson offers practical steps for creating a culture of transformational kindness through your approach to classroom management, relationships, assessment, and the content areas. She also demonstrates how to build kindness toward colleagues, parents, and families, and what to do in situations where supervisors are not so supportive. Finally, she describes how you can show more kindness toward yourself, including by giving grace.

Throughout this book, you'll find vignettes about the educators who have influenced their own communities through transformational kindness. You'll come away feeling inspired and encouraged to imagine a world in which schools are places where kindness and humanity are felt by all.

Hope E. Wilson is Professor of Education at the University of North Florida, USA. She has published over 50 peer-reviewed articles, book chapters, and research reports in the fields of gifted education and arts education. She is the co-author of the book *Letting Go of Perfect: Empowering Children to Overcome Perfectionism* (Routledge, 2021) with Dr. Jill Adelson.

Also Available from Routledge Eye On Education

(www.routledge.com/K-12)

Passionate Learners, Third Edition: How to Engage and Empower Your Students
Pernille Ripp

Everyday Self-Care for Educators: Tools and Strategies for Well-Being
Carla Tantillo Philibert, Christopher Soto, and Lara Veon

First Aid for Teacher Burnout, Second Edition: How You Can Find Peace and Success
Jenny Rankin

17 Things Resilient Teachers Do (And 4 Things They Hardly Ever Do)
Bryan Harris

Thank You, Teacher: 100 Uplifting and Affirming Letters from Your Fellow Educators
Brad Johnson and Hal Bowman

Safe, Seen, and Stretched in the Classroom: The Remarkable Ways Teachers Shape Students' Lives
Julie Hasson

Building Transformational Kindness in Schools

A Guide for Teachers and Leaders

Hope E. Wilson

NEW YORK AND LONDON

Cover image: © Getty Images

First published 2023
by Routledge
605 Third Avenue, New York, NY 10158, USA

and by Routledge
4 Park Square, Milton Park, Abingdon, Oxon, OX14 4RN, UK

Routledge is an imprint of the Taylor & Francis Group, an informa business.

ISBN: 978-1-032-16876-0 (hbk)
ISBN: 978-1-032-15764-1 (pbk)
ISBN: 978-1-003-25073-9 (ebk)

DOI: 10.4324/9781003250739

Typeset in Palatino
by SPi Technologies India Pvt Ltd (Straive)

Contents

Acknowledgments

I conceived of this book at the outbreak of the COVID-19 pandemic in 2020. As I watched the structures of the educational system strain in ways that we never could have anticipated and I witnessed the incredible power of teachers and school leaders to overcome them, I thought about all the caring teachers and mentors that I have had in my life. This book came out of those reflections and my hope for a future in which all students can experience care, compassion, and kindness in their educational journeys.

This book is dedicated to all the teachers, mentors, and supports in my life. And although I could not possibly name every educator who has molded me into the person I am today, I would like to specifically mention Dr. Diane Yendol-Hoppey and Dr. Jeffery Cornett at the University of North Florida, Dr. Del Siegle and Dr. Catherine Little at the University of Connecticut, Dr. Jane White and Dr. Barbara Sylvester at Austin College, Dr. Mary Christopher at Hardin-Simmons University, Ms. Linda Cook, Mr. Bruce MacDonald, Ms. Karen Kraft, and Ms. Kimberly Kass in my home school district in Coppell, Texas, and Dr. Jill Adelson, my best friend and emotional support since graduate school. I also want to thank every amazing teacher who has guided my own children as they make their way in the world, including Ms. Laurie Justo, Ms. Carrie McLeod, Ms. Isabella Araujo, Mr. Matt Peterson, Ms. Mollie Peterson, Ms. Lynsey McAninch, Mr. Jeff Grove, and Ms. Erica Sheehan. Thank you to everyone in my journey who has shown kindness, grace, and compassion to help my family and me reach our goals. This book is written to pass along your wisdom and kindness to the world.

Meet the Author

Dr. Hope (Bess) Wilson is a Professor of Education at the University of North Florida, where she oversees the graduate programs for the Teaching, Learning, and Curriculum Department and teaches Assessment and Educational Psychology. She has published over 50 peer-reviewed articles, book chapters, and research reports in the fields of gifted education and arts education. She is the co-author of the book *Letting Go of Perfect: Empowering Children to Overcome Perfectionism* (Routledge, 2021) with Dr. Jill Adelson. She is the past chair of the Research Evaluation Network and the Arts Network of the National Association for Gifted Children and Vice President for her local chapter of the United Faculty of Florida. She is the mother of two amazing children and spends her free time writing letters and making crafts for her friends and loved ones.

Introduction

At the beginning of each semester, I ask the freshmen in my *Introduction to the Teaching Profession* course to write down a memory of their best teacher during their years of schooling. I have been doing this activity since I started teaching at the university level over 15 years ago, but the results have not changed over time. Almost without exception, my students mention relationships—not curriculum, not assessments, not even the well-crafted lessons that their teachers spent hours creating. No, what my college-aged students remember about their best teacher is the relationship that the teacher fostered with them, the community they built in the classroom, the kindness that was shown. And that is what this book is about—how we, as the heart and soul of the schools, can make real change in the lives of our students, colleagues, and communities by adopting a framework of kindness. We can change our outlooks, mindsets, and paradigms to value kindness, to make our world, our communities, and our schools better places for the people who inhabit them.

Throughout this book, you will find vignettes about the teachers and school personnel who have influenced their educational communities through kindness. I encourage you to take the time as you read this book to remember that special teacher, mentor, or leader in your own life who made a difference in you. Reflect on the impact and how you can be that difference-maker for the people in your sphere of influence.

Throughout this book, I intentionally use "they/them/their" personal pronouns to acknowledge all people across the gender spectrum. I also use the more inclusive term "families" rather than parent or mother/father, to validate the multitude of people who come together to raise our children and students in our schools. I will use the term "educator" to refer to all professionals in a school system, from school staff to classroom teachers to school principals and administrators, to district or state level leaders, including instructors and professors in higher education. We all have a role to play in the education of students throughout our school systems.

This book will address systems of kindness, including kindness towards students, colleagues, communities, and self. My hope is that this book will inspire, motivate, and encourage you to imagine a world in which schools are places where kindness is felt by all.

1

What Is a Community of Kindness?

Imagine walking into a building every day where you feel loved and accepted for who you are, lifted to be the best version of yourself, and forgiven when you make mistakes.

Now imagine the opposite, a place where you feel excluded or unwelcome, punished for your mistakes, and expected to meet only the lowest of expectations.

In which scenario will you thrive? In this book, we will focus on building communities like the first example, built on systems of kindness, care, and compassion. But, just for a moment, I want you to imagine living in the second example, or perhaps you already do. When schools and the systems in which schools exist succumb to the pressures of accountability, lack of leadership, or the tensions of society, they can often adopt the mindset of scenario 2. It is no wonder that in 2019 over 2 million school-aged children had dropped out of school (Irwin et al., 2021), that close to a quarter of teachers in 2021 reported that they were likely to leave the profession (Steiner & Woo, 2021), or that almost 20% of high school students reported being bullied at school and over 37% reported feeling sad or hopeless most every day (CDC, 2019).

When school communities and systems fail to meet the basic human needs for relationships and affirmation, members are left with alienation and disconnection. This leads to a lack of motivation, which if left to fester and extend over a long period of time,

DOI: 10.4324/9781003250739-1

leads to burnout, dropout, and, at times, trauma. This is true for all students—those who are eager to please *and* those who are hard to like. This is true for all teachers in classrooms—those who are first to arrive/last to leave *and* those who are gone as soon as the last bell rings. This is true for all of the families at the school—those that volunteer for every committee on the PTA *and* those that only show up at school to complain. And this is true for all of the school administrators—those who lead from the heart *and* those who live by bureaucracy. In an ideal world, our school communities deliver kindness to each and every member, even the ones who make our lives more difficult.

Nice Versus Kind

In my favorite musical, *Into the Woods*, Little Red Riding Hood, in reflecting on her encounter with the Wolf, sings the line "Nice is different than good" (Stephen Sondheim). Among the genius and clever lines and wisdom from the composer Sondheim (and even in musical theater more generally), this advice is particularly poignant. In the musical, a young girl (Little Red) realizes that just because a stranger (the Wolf) is friendly, that does not mean that he has good intentions. And it leads me to a larger question when we discuss kindness and goodness: how are those ideas different from niceness? Clearly Sondheim is onto something.

To answer Sondheim's question, we can turn to another pop culture reference, one of my favorite movies, *Mean Girls*, and the book it was based on, *Queen Bees and Wannabes* (Wiseman, 2016). In the movie, written by Tina Fey, a new girl to school, Cady, has to navigate the world of teenage friendship at a suburban high school where she encounters the "Plastics" or popular, mean girls. This group, with their leader or Queen Bee, Regina, is at the top of the social ladder, and at first, Cady perceives them as nice. She soon sees through the façade of "fake niceness" to the cruel manipulations that underpin the female relationships in the movie. Cady is learning the difference between nice and kind.

Rosalind Wiseman, in her non-fiction book, explains in more depth the dynamics of adolescent female relationships in which there is a premium placed on appearing "nice" on the surface but using social power to bully, create cliques, and isolate others. In other words, being nice is a superficial characteristic, denoting perhaps politeness and socialized behavior. However, this niceness can mask cruel or harmful intentions, much in the way that Southern ladies are known to use "Bless your heart" when they do not approve of one's actions. They are superficially conveying a message of support or care, but the underlying message is one of disapproval.

Kindness, on the other hand, is the value that Cady finds at the end of *Mean Girls*, when she is named prom queen and shares her crown, not only with Regina but with all of the students at North Shore High. Kindness is genuine and complete. It encompasses both the outward action and the intent behind the action. When Cady shares her crown, she does not have an ulterior motive; she genuinely and completely cares for the other students at the school, regardless of their clique, social standing, or superficiality.

When someone acts out of kindness, they reveal a true regard for the humanity of the other person. It is an acknowledgement of true respect, care, and esteem for another. In short, kindness is doing good in the world because you care.

When we think about the systems in place at schools, the people who interact each day (faculty, staff, administrators, students, and families, finding kindness for the humanity of each person), we must reexamine all of the ways of work between people. We must focus on relationships.

What About People I Don't Like?

Sure, it's easy to show kindness to our BFF (best friend forever, for my readers who did not grow up in the 1990s) or our bestie (best friend, for my readers who aren't currently raising a teenager). As a teacher, you will find it easy to smile at the student who turns in their work, fully complete with beautiful handwriting.

It is not a challenge to say a nice word about a child to the family member who is volunteering to make your copies or hang up your bulletin boards. But what about those challenging co-workers, students, and families?

When a student has not completed their assigned work for the semester but would like you to give them extra credit, or a co-worker is heating up fish in the teachers' lounge microwave, we all struggle with how to be nice, much less kind. Even if as professionals we keep our composure and stay polite but later gossip about that co-worker (and, honestly, who hasn't?), then we are in the area of niceness and not kindness. And, trust me, I've been in that realm more than I would like to admit! If all of us are honest with ourselves, there are co-workers, faculty, staff, administrators, families, and even students that we like better than others. And some, quite frankly, that we probably dislike a great deal. So, what is an educator to do?

To be merely superficially nice is not sufficient; most of us can tell when a colleague is just being polite and not genuine. How many times have I heard "Nice shoes!" when I make questionable choices about my outfit? True intentions almost always come to the surface eventually, like when I notice the raised eyebrow that accompanies the "compliment" on my footwear.

Instead, we can focus on the humanity of the person that we struggle to like. You do not have to like their actions or even their personality, but try to remember your shared humanity with the person. By focusing on the things we have in common, our shared existence, we will find it easier to have kindness and work through disagreements. In upcoming chapters, we will discuss in more depth difficult colleagues and supervisors (Chapter 2), leadership (Chapter 3), classroom management and teaching (Chapter 4), and families (Chapter 5).

Note: this advice does not include working in abusive environments or relationships. Being kind to yourself (discussed in Chapter 5) includes protecting yourself from people who are physically, sexually, emotionally, or verbally abusive in the workplace. Although the signs of abuse are sometimes obvious (yelling, name-calling, and physical altercations), they are often more subtle (gaslighting, manipulation, and creating self-doubt).

It is outside of my areas of expertise to address this topic in this book, but if you suspect that you are in an abusive or unsafe environment, I encourage you to reach out to the organizations listed in the Resources section at the end of this book.

Accountability

> *When I imagine addressing a school's faculty members about radical and transformational kindness, I can envision waiting until the end of the session for* the question. *The hand that I know will be raised, maybe from a grizzled, experienced teacher or maybe from the fresh-faced recent College of Education graduate or even from an assistant principal or dean—but I know it is coming. They want to know about accountability. "How will be keep rigor?" or "Won't the students run all over us?" The faculty wants to know how we keep the members of our school communities accountable when we adopt kindness as our overarching framework.*

When it comes to school culture, we intuitively know that most everyone (school personnel, students, and families) responds to structure and guidelines, but we are often unsure of how high expectations interact with the framework of kindness. This recalls the earlier distinction between niceness and kindness. If you are being superficially nice, then you acquiesce to the status quo, avoiding confrontation to keep the peace and ignoring the ways in which the community is not living up to its potential. On the other hand, kindness dictates that we work with all parties to develop solutions, confronting the ways in which the expectations of the community are not being upheld. When we truly care about the people around us, we want to hold them to high standards, so they can fulfil their best possible outcomes.

That teacher who has shown a movie every class period for the last two weeks? We want to help them learn how to effectively write and implement lesson plans, so they can experience success as an instructor. What supports might they need? Additional resources from an experienced curricular coach? Family medical leave to care for a sick family member, so they do not have to try to juggle the work responsibilities with the care of family?

That student who could be heard from across the school building, yelling curse words at their teacher? We want to help them develop self-regulation skills, so they can communicate their needs effectively. What supports may this child need to express their emotions in a prosocial and productive way? Would they benefit from mental health and behavioral counseling? Could a social worker or interventionist help them cope with family or environmental stressors? Is there an unserved or unidentified exceptionality—such as attention-deficit/hyperactivity disorder (ADHD) or a learning disability—that is making school a stressful environment?

Being nice is eliminating all classwork and giving students a free day because we want students to like us. Being kind is knowing each student's strengths and weaknesses and holding them to high standards so they can experience the joy of achievement. Being unkind is punishing students with busywork because they were talking too much. Being kind is addressing the concern of distractions from chatter by classmates while working and developing structures that will help students work productively.

In short, it is kind to hold high standards while providing scaffolding to help community members reach those expectations.

In this chapter, we introduced the concept of kindness in school systems. In the following chapters, we will delve into specific relationships (students, colleagues, families, and communities) and situations facing school systems. I firmly believe that if we, as educational systems, can change the focus to building kindness and care for our fellow human beings, we can change the world.

You, as a member of the educational system, can affect your sphere of influence, whether that is a classroom, a school, an entire district, or even a single family. But one sphere at a time, we will change communities, and through those communities we will change the world. You do, indeed, have the most important responsibility in our society—to shape the future. Let's work together to make it a kinder one.

2

Kindness Towards Colleagues

At the beginning of the COVID-19 pandemic in 2020, our university (like institutions across the country) transitioned to remote instruction abruptly, directly after our spring break. I found myself suddenly isolated from my colleagues—the people who give me inspiration, challenge me to new heights, and encourage me when I have a difficult day. As the days turned into weeks and then into months, I could see the Zoom calls and virtual coffee chats weren't cutting it. I could see my department fraying at the seams, with the informal conversations in the hallways, the friendly banter at the coffee machine, the smiles in the parking lot; we were losing our good faith in each other. In addition, of course, we were facing some of the most challenging teaching situations of our careers: pivoting to virtual instruction with only a few days to really prepare, teaching students who were coping with illness, loss, and isolation. And, personally, the isolation of the pandemic was taking a toll on my own mental health. I could feel the depression settling in.

Something had to change. As was I looking around my bedroom-turned-home office, I remembered my childhood habit of writing letters and crafting gifts. So, I set about making small gifts for each person in my department—a personalized gift that would make them laugh or smile—along with a handwritten note telling them what makes them special and why they were important to our department. As I mailed these gifts, I found my own spirits lift. And over the course of the next several weeks, my colleagues reached out to me with their own stories of how this simple act of kindness arrived at a time that was particularly hard for them and how it made a difference in their lives. So, through the next year and a half, I continued my practice. Sometimes a postcard, sometimes a trinket, but always a handwritten note about why I think they are important and valuable. Spreading these acts of kindness helped make this little part of the world a better place.

As we think about the systems of schools and the incredible pressures put on those systems—not only a worldwide pandemic but limited funding, relatively low wages, increasing responsibilities and accountability, and critical shortages of personnel in many

DOI: 10.4324/9781003250739-2

areas—it is no wonder that relationships between co-workers become strained. If we conceptualize our schools as competitions—for limited resources, for the highest test scores, for the top evaluations—then we lose the ability to work together and make the entire system function under the framework of kindness. Unfortunately, sometimes the structures of local, state, and federal funding, the leadership at multiple levels, or our own frames of reference emphasize competition over kindness. This chapter will explore how we can change those mindsets and build relationships between colleagues within our school system.

As an educator, you'll find that the other educators in your building can be your greatest resource. When you are a new teacher, they can share lessons and ideas but also valuable information like how to fix the jam in the copy machine and the location of the closest adult restroom. As you become the experienced teacher, your colleagues become sources of new ideas, youthful energy, and excitement. In well-functioning schools, teachers form strong bonds and friendships over their shared experiences.

As a school or district leader, you'll find that your role may be different. Surely, relationships and trust are vital to maintain with your faculty, but friendship may (in some contexts) create dynamics of favoritism or prevent honest feedback in supervisory settings. So how to approach school leadership from an outlook of kindness? It certainly helps when kindness starts at the top.

And, finally, when we think about the colleagues in our school, do we include the staff? How does your school build relationships with the custodians, cafeteria servers and cooks, maintenance personnel, administrative assistants and bookkeepers, teacher assistants, security guards, and others? Each of these people is vital for the functioning of our schools and yet often feel on the outside. How can we widen our circle to bring them into our community?

When we change our focus to kindness and building relationships with everyone in our school the community thrives. We find teachers working together (across disciplines and levels), leaders and teachers communicating about needs and strengths, and staff being included in the decision-making process. The school becomes a place that people want to come to each day. Mondays are not quite so dreadful, and the teachers' lounge is a happy place to spend some time.

Working with Your Supervisor

> *From the first day in my new department over 10 years ago, I knew it was different. All of my new colleagues seemed to get along, to support one another, and department meetings felt more like friendly gatherings to share ideas than anything else. We shared as many laughs as meeting minutes, and all voices (even those of a newly minted assistant professor) were heard. As I became more acculturated to my new surroundings, I realized that this environment was carefully cultivated by our department chair, Dr. Jeffery Cornett. His core value of unconditional positive regard for everyone permeated every aspect of our way of work and compelled all of us to be our very best. Each morning, I could look forward to a friendly conversation with my boss as he took time from his busy day to stop and chat at my office door. He shared this value to all in our department from distinguished full professors to the administrative staff to the custodians. Everyone knew they were a valued part of our team because of the way that our chair interacted with us, and because of this, we all treated each other with respect as well. Even when we disagreed about policy or the curriculum (as academics often do), we never lost respect for each other or disvalued the work that we each contributed to the department. This leadership made Dr. Cornett a boss who was easy to work for and a leader that I still strive to be in my own life.*

As an educator of any rank, we all have leaders or administrators that we must report to—whether that is a principal, dean, department chair, or superintendent. When we are lucky, we have a leader who builds us up, believes that we can accomplish great things, and provides quality feedback so we can improve. But, sometimes, we find ourselves in situations in which our direct supervisors leave much to be desired. In either case, as part of the school system, how do we demonstrate radical and transformational kindness to our supervisors?

Finding the Right Fit

When I was interviewing for a teaching position in my hometown, I arrived early to the school for my interview. This was my typical practice, to allow some time to observe the school office and get a feel for the environment of the school. It was the end of the school day and the usual controlled chaos of an elementary school was present, but I took note of the smiles from the bookkeeper and the school nurse manning the front desk and how they seemed to know each and every student's name. Then, a girl walked in with a broken sandal in her hand—in tears because she did not know how she was going to walk home without a shoe. I watched as the school principal, Mr. Bruce MacDonald, took the time out of his day (knowing he had an appointment scheduled with me for the interview) to stop and help. After assessing the situation and knowing the neighborhood—the girl lived just a few streets down from the school—he produced a stapler from his office and stapled her sandal back together. He reassured her that she could make it home but also that if she had a problem, he would still be at the school to help. And like that, she was on her way. Even though I had to wait a few extra minutes for our interview to start, I knew this was the school where I wanted to teach!

The first kindness is to the system and to yourself, by, when possible, selecting healthy work environments that have leaders who can foster kindness in their spheres of influence.

When selecting a new job and going to an interview, you should remember that you are evaluating them as much as they are evaluating you. Ask yourself if this is a place where the leadership values the community and kindness is at the forefront of the decision-making process. A community of kindness is best situated when the values are supported, expected, and modeled from the top.

Of course, we do not always have the luxury of being selective on which position that we accept. We might be place-based with limited choices for job opportunities or chose places of employment for other reasons (shorter commutes, opportunities for family members, increased salary, etc.), or we could be facing a tight job market in which any job offer is well worth employment. Or we can accept a job only to find out that the leader who hired you is replaced by someone who does not have the same values.

The first step to building a relationship with your supervisor is to see them as a fellow human being who has strengths and weaknesses and is worthy of care and compassion. This means they will not always be perfect and will certainly make mistakes in their role, and you will not always understand the decisions that they make. But, in a healthy work environment, you will be able to build trust and ask for the rationale behind decisions, bring concerns to your supervisor, and expect support in return. At the same time, you can also demonstrate transformational kindness by taking the time to share what you appreciate about their leadership decisions, actions, and work. By showing your support and gratitude, you can work to build up the good will and support for times when you need to bring up concerns.

How to Show Support

If you are genuinely expressing your appreciation, rather than paying compliments to get ahead, then you are demonstrating true kindness. This is the distinction between flattery and kindness—intention. If your motive is to truly compliment and raise the spirit of your supervisor rather than to promote your own agenda, then you are fostering a compassionate work environment.

There is a delicate balance between "bootlicking" and being sincere to your supervisor, and you certainly do not want the reputation of being a suck-up. Again, the answer here is nice versus kind and intent. Most of us can differentiate between a sincere compliment based on specific evidence and insincere and inane platitudes. When giving your supervisor a compliment, be sure to connect it to a specific incident and find something that you genuinely appreciate about them. I find this particularly effective when I know it was a difficult decision or problem to be solved. For example, how they handled an irate parent, mediated a dispute between colleagues, or found funding for an important initiative. When appropriate, this can be written—a short note in a mailbox or even an email with their boss carbon copied.

How to Address Concerns

Other times, you will be hurt by decisions, feedback, or interactions with your supervisor. Figuring out how to mediate this conflict is difficult because of the obvious power differential. When viewing this conflict or hurt through the lens of kindness, we would first want to consider this conflict as unintentional or serving a greater good for the community, unless there is direct evidence to the contrary. In other words, transformational kindness would direct us to give our supervisor the benefit of the doubt.

Given this assumption, our logical next step would be to arrange a time to clear the air, preferably in person, in which facial expressions and tone of voice can fully express the nuance of emotions. Too often, written communication in these instances can miscommunicate intent. However, written communication may be preferable if you want documentation of the conversation, if scheduling time is difficult, or if you want to be able to carefully plan your words ahead of time. If you do choose written communication, be sure that you have allowed yourself to calm down and process strong emotions before sending the email, text, or note. It is also helpful to have a loved one, trusted colleague, or outside individual read your communication before sending, to ensure that your message is clearly conveyed and that your message can be received with the intention that you are sending.

In any case, it is helpful to begin the conversation, whether in person or in writing, with a reminder of the goodwill and goals that you share (e.g., creating a healthy learning or working environment, student success, and/or the mission of the school). Then you can describe the incident and why it is concerning to you. Try to be as objective as possible in the description and explanation of the effects on you, your students, or the school. Finally, end with what steps you would like them to take. This might be a request for an explanation for the decision, an assurance that it will be avoided in the future, or a way to restore the circumstances and repair the situation or change to policy or procedures. Keep in mind that they may not be able to accommodate your request, or they may have an alternate solution. Hopefully, this will start a dialog that will lead to a mutually agreeable solution.

In offering possible solutions, you are communicating to your supervisor that you are invested in finding a resolution. Although they are likely the ultimate decision maker in the situation, you can communicate your perspective and commitment to the functioning of the school environment. This further communicates the idea that you are on the same team and that you want to work towards resolving the conflict.

The goals of this conversation are to:

1. Begin with shared goals and understandings
2. Share your concerns
3. Offer possible solutions
4. Discuss ways to move forward

In the discussion of ways to move forward, you may come to realize that your supervisor was considering factors outside of your sphere when making the decision. While you may not like the outcome, you may have to accept the solution. For example, if the state changed the regulations about testing schedules, you may have to move the date of the annual field day celebration. On the other hand, as you discuss the issue with your supervisor, the two of you may be able to develop a solution that is better than what either of you could have devised on your own. For example, after hearing your concerns about the field day, together you could combine it with the PTA end-of-year celebration and have an event that includes the entire community later in the semester.

Now What?

What if your discussion with your supervisor does not work and no resolution is reached? Sometimes our supervisors are not reasonable people, or the disagreements are on a deep philosophical level that cannot be resolved. I once worked for a principal whom I never saw leave her office but who still gave me an unsatisfactory evaluation on my annual report. You can imagine my outrage, especially as a young and inexperienced teacher full of self-righteousness!

When your informal conversation does not reach a satisfactory resolution, you do have several options, all of which might be the kindest option, depending on the circumstances:

1. Drop the issue and move on.
2. Leave the situation or work environment.
3. Continue to fight the situation.

The kindest option might be to drop the matter and move on within your sphere of influence. You can learn from the experience and try not to put yourself in a similar situation in the future, or you could decide that this conflict is not worth your time and energy. This can preserve your own mental health, to be able to move on from the incident. In more extreme cases, you may lose some respect for your supervisor, and it may be that kindness will not flow from the top down at your school system. You can still work on spreading kindness from your own sphere of influence, among your colleagues and to your students.

On the other hand, the kindest move might be to remove yourself from the environment. To be kind to yourself, you might need to leave a toxic workplace or boss. This is most likely the course of action after a pattern of incidents, or if the conflict is unresolvable and threatens your livelihood, mental or physical health, or your safety. It is not in the scope of this book to detail the traits of unhealthy and unsafe work environments, but in the Resources section, you will find places to research more information. Do not feel afraid to leave a place that is detrimental to your mental health.

Finally, the kindest action for the school system as a whole or for your own sense of accomplishment might be to fight the decision. You may want to reach out to your local teachers' union (see Resources section) to help with the process if it concerns your contract, legal issues (e.g., unjust labor practices), or policies that could be changed at the district or state levels. You may also want to gather support from your colleagues who feel similarly about the issue, as there is strength in numbers.

The first step in this process is to gather your documentation, including taking notes or saving the response to your first conversation. For further support, you can email the notes to your supervisor and ask them to confirm that this is what you spoke about. (Even if they do not respond, now they are part of a written record.) The next action is to make a second, polite, but firm, request for resolution. When you feel that it is appropriate, you can bring your boss's supervisor into the conversation. If you are working with your teachers' union, they likely have a similar process to follow. The human resources department of your institution might also have guidelines for disputes.

When you work to make your workplace a better place by resolving conflicts and fighting for the best interests of you, your colleagues, and your students, you are working to make the school system a kinder place. Activism is an important part of kindness.

Building a Relationship With Your Supervisor

But, in my experience, most supervisors are somewhere on the continuum from absolutely amazing to completely toxic—meaning that they make mistakes and let me down, but we also have a shared vision and work together to make our school a better place to learn. Thus, we can, and must, work together to build a working relationship with a foundation of kindness. As an educator, you can do this by adding goodwill, starting from a place of trust, and honestly bringing concerns as they arise.

Communities of Practice

> As I entered the school where I ended my K-5 teaching career, in large letters on the wall was our school motto—"It Matters To Me What Happens To You!"—and surrounding it were construction paper cutouts of the American Sign Language sign for "I love you" with every

> child's signature. For most schools, this would have been a lovely display, something for parents and community members to smile at when they walked to the office, but not much more. But, at Mockingbird Elementary School, this was our way of life. From our principal (remember Mr. MacDonald from the previous section?) to the youngest kindergartener, everyone took the time to care about each other. If a child saw a piece of trash on the playground, they immediately picked it up to throw away, knowing that it was everyone's responsibility to keep our school clean for the community. If a child was crying in the hallway, any adult would stop to comfort them—even the custodian or the fifth-grade reading coach. And this care permeated to the relationships between colleagues and teachers at the school—I have never experienced such collaboration between and across departments, grade levels, and classrooms.

As educators, we are in a unique working environment. On one hand, we spend most of our day in our own classroom, in which we have relative independence with little contact with other adults. On the other hand, we work collaboratively with grade level or content area teams to plan and learn together. Classroom teachers must also collaborate with the special education teachers and paraprofessionals, the English language learner support faculty and staff, the teachers' aides and paraprofessionals, the "specials teachers" (art, music, physical education, etc.), and the numerous other professionals in our building. We function both independently and collaboratively, and navigating these juxtapositions comes to the heart of our professions.

As I have grown as an educator over my career and in my current role as a teacher educator, I have come to appreciate the power of communities of practice and the collaboration of educators. And, when viewed through the lens of kindness, these communities of practice have the potential to change teaching in schools today. We all need the support and kindness of our colleagues and the surprising gratification we get when we spread that kindness to others.

Unconditional Positive Regard

Rogers (1957), the first researcher to use the term, defines unconditional positive regard in terms of the therapist/client relationship like this:

> "It involves as much feeling of acceptance for the client's expression of negative, 'bad,' painful, fearful, defensive, abnormal feelings as for his expression of 'good,' positive, mature, confident, social feelings, as much acceptance of ways in which he is inconsistent as of ways in which he is consistent. It means caring for the client, but not in a possessive way or in such a way as simply to satisfy the therapist's own needs. It means a caring for the client as a separate person, with permission to have his own feelings, his own experiences".
>
> (p. 225)

In short, unconditional positive regard indicates that we respect each person as a human being with perspectives, options, and feelings of their own. As we consider our colleagues and fellow educators, unconditional regard is the starting point. It means recognizing that our co-workers have strengths and weaknesses, good and bad days, room for growth, and diverse backgrounds we may not understand. Of course, this is easy for our work besties, the teacher down the hall that we share drinks with after a hard week or who brings us an iced latte on Monday morning. But can we extend this regard to our grumpy classroom neighbor, the teacher who shows up for after-school duty late more than they are on time, or the colleague who just never seems to be all that friendly? It helps to remember that we are all human, and we do not always know everyone's back story, what challenges they are facing in their classroom or personal life, or differences in personality. We certainly do not have to be best friends with everyone in the building, but it helps to have unconditional positive regard for their humanity.

One way I have experienced this in my own workspace is the vignette at the beginning of this chapter. When I noticed the department (or school in your case, perhaps) was going through a particularly difficult or stressful time, I took the time to write a note to each member of our shared community. This gave me an opportunity to reflect on the unique contribution that each person brought to our workplace. By thinking of each one separately, I was able to appreciate them as individuals on a deeper level. To increase the value you are able to see in each person, the gesture does not have to be as big—it could be a few words on a sticky note—or done for everyone all at once. You might try to spread one kind gesture a day (or week).

If you do not feel comfortable writing notes or giving gifts, you could try a smile and a kind word in the hallway. Or you could practice this as a thought exercise. Think of each member of your educational community and what unique and positive contribution they make to the workplace. You can make a list, mentally or written out, of these characteristics. As you do this, you will feel your attitude and outlook towards your colleagues change for the better.

Once you have unconditional positive regard for your fellow educators or are working towards that goal, your actions will naturally follow. You will find yourself quicker with a smile, less often annoyed with minor inconveniences, and better able to work in teams. Remember, you are acting with integrity and true kindness, not the façade of niceness.

Shared Goals

Another tool in the building of communities of practice is the concept of shared goals. As educators in a school system, we are working towards a common vision and outcomes—to educate the students in our schools and make our school a better place to work and learn. Even when we disagree on the best methods to accomplish these goals, we can typically agree on common ground of our shared purpose. When conflict arises, it is helpful to remember that we are working towards a shared vision. As your community of practice deepens relationships, these goals can become more specific. For example, your group may be able to agree on a foundation of kindness for approaching all aspects of systems within the school. Starting each term, year, or significant change to the school structure with a session to develop shared goals can help facilitate this process and help build common understandings and school culture.

Giving Grace

One thing that I am particularly guilty of is holding people (specifically my work colleagues) to exceptionally high standards. This can be a good thing, as it can raise expectations and allow everyone to shine and challenge the group to be their best. However, on bad days, it can mean that I am overly critical and unforgiving. When a colleague does not meet my expectations of them, whether that be foundational (like a pedagogical difference in how to teach a concept) or more pedantic (like skipping in front of me in the queue for the copy machine), I tend to lay the blame on others' fundamental faults. I am far from perfect.

However, when I view the world through the lens of transformational kindness, I can recognize my colleagues' humanity. I can see that there might be more than one way to teach a concept, that everyone has bad days, and that sometimes all of us are running late and need to make copies ASAP. In short, through kindness, I am able to give grace and forgiveness to my co-workers' occasional missteps or philosophical differences. By respecting them as people, I can recognize that we are all imperfect and worthy of forgiveness.

Mediating Conflict

Sometimes, however, the offending behavior is repeated or intentional. While I can give grace to the teacher who is late to afterschool duty on occasion, after a full week of tardiness, I may no longer be willing to give up my precious planning time to cover for them. Just like conflict with supervisors, most of these conflicts are best resolved with a short, in-person conversation, in which you can reiterate your mutual respect and shared goals and then address the concern, focusing on a resolution. Through this conversation, you may learn more about the situation that can help you be empathetic towards the colleague or discover a structural problem that you can work collaboratively to solve. The keys to these conversations are to build upon positive interactions you have shared and to address the source of conflict as directly as possible. Demonstrating your unconditional regard for your colleague through your words can go a long way in dissolving any tension.

Now What?

Of course, a calm conversation is not always possible when you find yourself with a toxic colleague. And sometimes, even after the conversation, the behavior does not change. In either situation, it is important to document your concerns through written communication. The next step is to involve your supervisor or human resource office to help mediate the conflict. Again, it is up to you to decide when (or if) to escalate the conflict by involving outside or supervisory parties. It might be the kindest course of action to you and the school system as a whole to set the conflict aside and move on. Or it might be the kindest course of action to pursue a change.

Building Community

As an educator, you are ultimately empowered to build the community at your school. Community comes from kind actions: sincere compliments, random acts, and giving grace. These can be intentional, like organized happy hours and social functions, or organic, like smiles in the hallway and conversation around the coffee machine. Community is built by celebrating large and small victories and by offering support in challenging times.

There is no one I want working with me through the journey of teaching than my fellow teachers. They have the combined knowledge, expertise, enthusiasm, encouragement, and skills to change the world.

3

Kindness Through Leadership

A few years ago, I was asked to give the opening address to the teachers at Terry Parker High School in my county. When I arrived at the school, the cafeteria was covered in large posters with each teacher's name in large print. Underneath their name, each of the administrators had written a personal note about what that person brings to the school and their positive qualities. For the rest of the day, the teachers were invited to add to each of the posters, contributing to the affirming words for each member of the community. As I interacted with the faculty for the remainder of my day, I was struck by the vision of the leadership and how they set the stage for the entire school year. Not only did they take the time to honor and recognize each member of the faculty, but they also modeled the actions and encouraged the entire group to continue the practice.

It is my sincere hope that every teacher has the opportunity to work under the leadership of a principal who values kindness. Thinking back to Mr. MacDonald from previous vignettes, I recall that he truly made a school that was a joy to enter each day and a community that welcomed people with open arms. But unpacking the leadership and the community he set is a bit more complicated. How can we, as school leaders, be more like Mr. MacDonald or the leadership at Terry Parker? What does leadership look like in the lens of kindness?

As a school leader, whether that is as a teacher-leader, department lead, assistant principal, head of school, academic coach, or other title, you have a variety of job responsibilities, to the teachers, to the students and their families, and to the school boards and superintendents. These roles all come with high

DOI: 10.4324/9781003250739-3

expectations, stress, and long hours, but to change the systems of schools for the better, we must approach them with the lens of kindness. When we take this approach, we also find that the school becomes a place where we enjoy being and the stress is lessened.

Building Relationships

> During the COVID-19 pandemic, my favorite dean started hosting virtual coffee chats for the faculty to stop in, ask questions, and raise concerns. After about a month, I happened to pop into the chat. I found my dean, alone in the chat, waiting for anyone to show up. It was at that moment that I realized the vulnerability of being a school leader and the struggle to find relationships and friendship when you are at the top. It is indeed lonely.

If you are new to a leadership position, you may be nervous about how relationships change as you move into a supervisory role. Certainly, how the power dynamics have changed and easy friendship between teachers do not easily translate to teachers and supervisors. It can be lonely at the top.

If you are an experienced leader but are in a new position, you may face a faculty that is wary of the new leader. Perhaps you are replacing a beloved administrator, or you are just the latest in a series of seemingly replaceable personnel. It can be difficult to build trust and relationships in either situation. It certainly will not happen overnight.

Or perhaps you have been in your position for years. Maybe it is going fine, but you know it could be better. Or maybe you have lost the trust of your faculty and staff. How can you repair those relationships and build back trust?

It is true that relationship-building between leadership and faculty will not be the same as between faculty colleagues. And the degree of difference will vary depending on the level of supervisory responsibility the leader has over the faculty, thus affecting the power differential. The person completing the personnel evaluations will have a different relationship with the teachers they are evaluating than the academic coach who supports teacher growth by co-teaching lessons and modeling best practice with no supervisory evaluations. But, it is vital that, as a leader, you develop kind relationships with every faculty and staff member under your care. You may find that your friendships reorient to focus more towards others at your same level of leadership (e.g., other principals, heads of schools, and deans).

To build relationships with faculty and staff through the lens of kindness, the key elements are the following:

- **Unconditional positive regard**: Remembering and treating each member of the community as valuable
- **Fairness**: Treating each person with equity, allocating resources according to need and without bias
- **Trust**: Mutual understanding that each party will act with integrity
- **Authenticity**: Being your true self in front of faculty and staff, including admitting mistakes
- **Transparency**: Providing rationale and reasons for decisions that are made

In the next sections, I will elaborate on each of these principles and how they apply to the work of an educational leader.

Unconditional Regard

Can you recognize the strengths and value of each member of your faculty and staff? Even those with poor performance or negative attitudes? As a leader, you are responsible for setting the tone for your community. And by taking the time to recognize the value of each individual, like the leadership at Terry Parker High School, you can change the climate of your school. You can accomplish this through "shout-outs" in faculty meetings or emails, short notes put in mailboxes, or a kind word in the hallways.

When you have a faculty member with poor performance or a negative attitude, good leaders quickly realize that this one person can have a domino effect on an entire school community.

And if this person is truly unhappy at your school, then ignoring the problem is not a kindness towards your community or the individual themselves.

The first step to resolving this conflict is communication—as is usually the case with conflict. If you have already built a relationship of trust, you may be able to ask the faculty member why they are unhappy or their performance is slipping directly. If you are facing a more contentious situation, begin by finding common ground (e.g., the school mission, successful school year, or the best interest of the teacher). Then the two of you can work together to find a solution.

Through this conversation, you may find out that the faculty member is facing a personal or family obstacle, making their work more challenging. You can help connect them to resources through Human Resources, such as an Employee Assistance Program (EAP), which provides free short-term counseling to employees. You may also be able to provide community resources, such as those listed in the Resources section at the end of the book. If nothing else, communicate your empathy for them, and you may be able to adjust some work responsibilities temporarily as they cope with the crisis.

On the other hand, you may find that the troubled faculty member does not have the requisite skill set for their given job. Perhaps the teacher is not suited for their current grade level or content area, or maybe they have been asked to address students with specific needs (e.g., exceptionalities, giftedness, or English language learners) for which they do not have the background experience. Maybe they are new graduates of a teacher preparation program, or they are on a temporary certificate, and they do not have some foundational lesson planning, pedagogical, or classroom management skills.

When a teacher is struggling, it is important that, as a leader, you are kind and offer support to help them gain the skills they need. You might be able to provide a substitute teacher so they can observe an expert teacher for a day or attend a Professional Learning opportunity. An academic coach in your building or a new teacher mentor in your district could come in to co-teach a few lessons and offer support. You could also provide

Professional Learning workshops, self-studies, or books as additional ways to support the teacher. In this conversation, be sure that you establish a separation between your role as an evaluator and your supportive role. In this case, you should be concentrating on building relationships and providing resources and help—remembering your unconditional human regard for your teacher. The best outcome will be a faculty member who experiences success and has a change in attitude—ready to approach new challenges with confidence.

At other times, you may realize that the best solution for the functioning of your school is to reorganize. Perhaps your fifth-grade teacher needs a change of pace and wants to venture into first grade. Or a beloved second grade teacher is going to move up with their current students to third grade. Maybe the algebra teacher completed their training and is ready to teach the Advanced Placement courses. As a school leader, you get to put together the fascinating puzzle of the unique talents of your faculty and match their skills to their roles. You can identify potential in a teacher before they see it in themselves, and your encouragement and support will lead them to higher achievement and happiness in their career.

Finally, at the end of the day, there may be some teachers, faculty, or staff who are not a good match for the profession or for your school. This is not a conclusion that can be determined lightly or quickly, except in drastic circumstances (e.g., a felony crime, assault, and theft). However, after supportive actions and both positive and direct communications have failed to change the patterns of behavior of the faculty, the kindest action may be to direct the faculty member to a new career path. I have seen excellent school leaders have conversations with teachers, acknowledging the situation and providing guidance in selecting a new area for employment. Honestly, the teachers left the meeting in which they were terminated from employment with a mutually agreed-upon good will and pleasant parting. Although I probably lack the finesse and skill to have the conversation go quite as smoothly, the principle of the conversation is the same. How can we help all members of the community benefit from a decision that is kind to the community?

If a teacher is consistently violating the school policy, community norms, and/or ethics of behavior, it is vital to document each instance, to communicate to the faculty member that policies were violated and how to remedy the situation, and to prepare if termination of employment is needed. Remember that keeping ineffective or negative teachers who cannot or will not change at a school is not kind to the students, the other faculty members, or the teacher themselves. They may be equally unhappy with their current employment situation, experiencing feelings of inadequacy at their poor performance, and/or unfulfilled with their career. A nudge from you might be the motivation that they need to explore positive changes in their life.

Before you take formal disciplinary action, it is usually more kind to approach the situation informally. A face-to-face, frank conversation about the faculty's performance can be supportive and help resolve the situation. Unless their behavior endangers students or other members of the community. In this case, document the incident(s) and go through the formal channels immediately. This could include revoking of a teaching license, legal actions, or immediate administrative leave/termination. It is imperative that you keep your school community and children safe.

Fairness

Fairness in leadership does not necessarily mean that every faculty member and staff gets the same support, attention, and assignments. Rather, fairness means that everyone gets what they need to be successful and for a well-functioning community of practice. For example, a teacher who is given more classes to prepare may also need more time to plan in comparison with a teacher who teaches the same content all day long. A novice teacher may need more professional learning opportunities or direct instruction than a teacher who has many years of experience. Certainly, not every teacher in your building needs the same professional learning experience. An extroverted teacher may be best suited to be the advisor for the spirit club, while a more reserved teacher may be better suited for other administrative tasks.

In considering the strengths of each member of your school community, be mindful of those who volunteer too often and get burned out from too much work or those who are waiting to be asked. It is okay if the work is not equally spread out across the team, but it should be as equitable as possible, considering each member's strengths and weaknesses. And additional work should be compensated appropriately, as a teachers' contract allows.

Trust

All relationships are built on trust. As a supervisor, you may have to work hard to gain the trust of your faculty and staff. This will take time, as the community is witness to your integrity. You must live the way in which you speak, living up to the standards that you hold for your faculty and staff. You must keep the confidentiality of faculty, staff, students, and families. And you must treat everyone with kindness. Be patient—as the community sees your character, the trust will grow.

Remember that trust is a two-way street. You can also build trust by trusting your faculty and staff. If you approach each interaction, each school year, and each incident with positive regard, assuming that you are working with a professional who has studied their craft, your faculty and staff will recognize the trust you place in them. And, step by step, the trust will grow. Mutual trust is a key component of a functional, and kind, school community.

It can be scary for you, as a leader, to give up control, to stop micromanaging, and to rely and trust the faculty and staff at a school. When we, as leaders, can put our trust in teachers to act responsibly, act with integrity, and work in the best interests of the community, we build kindness and trust in our community.

Authenticity

Okay, all that about trust sounds great. But what happens when I make a mistake? What happens if I do not act with integrity on occasion? What if I am (gasp) not perfect?

The good news is none of us is perfect—and if we were, our faculty and staff probably would not trust us anyway. The key is to act with authenticity when we do make a mistake.

My favorite dean of all time, Dr. Diane Yendol-Hoppey, is expert at authenticity. When she joined our faculty seven years ago, it was her first deanship, and we were a deeply divided community. She had a lot of work to do and huge changes to make, and not all her decisions were perfect. But, at every turn, she was ready to admit when she made a misstep and ask for forgiveness. I can only imagine the bravery it would take to face a room full of professors (who are generally known to be pretty head-strong and opinionated) and say that you were not right and ask for their forgiveness. And, yet, this female scholar, a true leader, won over our college faculty and staff by never being anyone other than herself. She has guided us by her vision, showed up her emotions when appropriate, and apologized as necessary. And, in turn, I trust her judgment and will follow her lead.

Transparency

Now, if you ask Dr. Yendol-Hoppey about transparency, she will say she does not like it when faculty use that term. However, I like to remind her that she leads our college with a great deal of transparency—with the trust that she has built through her authenticity, we can believe that the decisions she makes for the college (even when we do not agree with them) are the best for the community. But, most importantly, she is open to explaining her reasoning to anyone who asks. When it comes to disruptive changes, she proactively describes her rationale and how it is in the best interests of our community of practice as a whole.

This has done wonders to quell rumors among faculty and build a common sense of purpose. I have heard more than one faculty member comment that although a decision does not benefit them directly or they do not agree with it, they understand why it was made. As a school leader, Dr. Yendol-Hoppey has to report to many different groups—the community, her supervisors, the faculty, our students—but she has built the faculty trust by explaining how her decisions impact each of the constituencies. This level of transparency requires vulnerability and authenticity, to open yourself up to criticism and explain your reasoning. However, by including everyone in your thought processes and decision-making, you build community and trust.

Developing Communities of Kindness

> The name of my current department is "Teaching, Learning, and Curriculum" or "TLC." I particularly love this title because it could also mean "Tender Loving Care"—a value that I see our faculty exude every day! Owing to the leadership of our department chairs and dean, we have the opportunity to spend time with each other, celebrating our mutual and individual successes, grieving together during hardships, and relying on each other to overcome the hard times.

As a school leader, you have the unique opportunity to situate your community in a way that develops and demonstrates kindness to the world. By focusing on the welcoming culture, the hiring and retention process, giving feedback, and your school policies, you can create a community of kindness in your educational institution.

Welcoming Environment and Culture

As a leader in your school community, you have the unique position to set the tone for your group. Your leadership guides how members interact with each other and how new people are inducted into the community. As important as it is for teachers to welcome their students into the classrooms with a warm smile, how do you greet your staff and faculty each morning? Do you take the time to greet the students, faculty, and staff during the morning announcements or at the parent drop-off? Do not discount the importance of consistent, small gestures to change the tone and environment of an entire school community.

The front office of any school is the first interaction that most people have with your school, whether that be prospective teachers, families, or students transferring to your school. The staff that you have in those key roles is vital to conveying the values of your school community. When I was a kindergartener at Richard J. Lee Elementary School, I thought the school secretary was the most beautiful person in the world. For me, she hung the moon, because she treated everyone—even the smallest kindergartener with crazy red hair—with love and respect.

When you have new faculty and staff, how do you model a welcoming community? A community-wide email is nice, but a personal introduction, particularly to key personnel and those you encounter in the hallway on your tour of the school, is transformational kindness. What welcome do new students and families get to your community? Remember that families are entrusting you with the most valuable parts of their hearts—how do you welcome them into your community? What about substitute teachers, maintenance workers, pre-service teachers and interns, or paraprofessionals?

When the leader of a school takes the time to welcome every new member of the community with open arms, the entire community can feel more secure in their place in it. This spirit helps make your school a place where everyone is celebrated and wants to be.

You can accomplish this by being present. Make it a point to be visible and active during high-traffic times of the day (e.g., arrival/dismissal and lunch). Welcome all community members with a genuine smile and a warm greeting. This is how you develop relationships. Having unconditional positive regard, take care to show the same respect to staff (custodians, maintenance workers, cafeteria service professionals, and paraprofessionals) as faculty. Spend extra time building relationships with those members of your community who seem the most on the outside, bringing them into your circle and helping them find a place in your group.

Some leaders have found success with team-building activities. Although personally I sometimes find these artificial and without purpose, they can also be powerful ways to develop common experiences and find personal connections. You are in the best position to know your community and whether they are amenable to these approaches. You could suggest, as an alternative, an activity with a common purpose. This could be a service activity for the local community or school, developing a vision or mission for the school, or team planning.

Hiring and Retention

> In my department, Dr. Rick Chant has been on every single hiring committee for the last 15 years. We jokingly credit him for the success and cohesiveness of our department faculty. In fact, his wisdom has guided our department in selecting excellent faculty over the last 15 years, and we all recognize that his contribution to our work is immeasurable. He has a knack for instantly understanding how a candidate will fit with the rest of our colleagues and finding the perfect match to our needs.

As an educational leader, you are in the unique position to build your community through the hiring process. In fact, this may be the most important task you have in shaping the community of your school. As we are facing record-breaking teacher shortages across the country (NCES, 2022), you may also be struggling to fill the positions that you have open at your school. In considering the hiring process through the lens of kindness, you are looking for candidates who will be successful in the challenges and environment of your school—a person that you can nurture and who will grow into the role.

Fundamentally, you are seeking a person who shares the vision of the school and is open to learn and grow in skills to continue to be successful. Keep in mind that this person may not necessarily be the one with the most qualifications on their resumé or be the smoothest speaker in the interview.

In a kindness-focused interview, the questions are designed to get to know each candidate rather than to "catch" them in something that they do not know. Remember that the candidate that you most want likely has job offers from other schools, so your interview must also convince them that your community is a good fit for them.

In the current state of education, school leaders are facing teacher shortages: in 2022, more than 45% of schools reported at least one vacancy halfway through the school year (NCES, 2022). This can lead school leaders to hire any "warm body" to fill the position. However, I strongly caution against this approach, despite the overwhelming pressures. From the kindness lens, you are looking for a leader in your community who will uphold the values, treat all with respect, and have the competence to effectively teach your students. You may do better by cultivating a strong cohort of long-term substitute teachers who can fill in until a full-time, certified teacher can be found. Additionally, developing relationships with nearby colleges of education and teacher preparation programs can help to provide a source of candidates for openings. For example, openings in the fall and winter can be filled by students who graduate in December.

The flip side to strategic hiring is retention of your most valuable resources: the members of your community. Of course, the relationship-building detailed in the first part of this chapter is the key to keeping faculty and staff. With trust and open communication, you can develop a sense of when faculty and staff are becoming dissatisfied with their work.

However, it is also helpful to be more purposeful in your collection of feedback. The leadership in my college set up an email account where we can submit ideas and solutions for issues and problems that we encounter. This has empowered faculty and staff to be solution-focused and to take ownership of our community. I also suggest regular anonymous feedback surveys sent to members of your educational community (faculty, staff, and parents) regarding leadership. This exercise can help you understand your own weaknesses and areas for growth. It can also highlight structural issues in your school that can impede growth of community. Although receiving feedback can be difficult, especially when it is negative, it also provides the impetus for personal growth and change. And providing the opportunity to your school community to provide feedback helps to develop trust, particularly when they see how you use the information gathered to make meaningful change to your own leadership style—with authenticity and transparency.

Giving Feedback

Another key job responsibility of school leaders is to evaluate and give feedback to faculty and staff. Many members of school communities have experience with this process only as punitive, focusing on ways to highlight mistakes and to harm teachers. Others have received only glowing feedback, with no meaningful ways to improve and grow professionally. Neither approach is kind to faculty.

Just as we must be honest in providing feedback to students, we must be honest in evaluating faculty and staff—giving a realistic appraisal of whether they have met the standards of satisfactory performance. For teachers or staff who have not met these standards, this may (understandably) be difficult news to deliver, but that is why you make the big bucks—just kidding. But, the truth about their performance is the kindest path forward—for the students, for the other staff and faculty, and, ultimately, for the faculty member themselves. By documenting their performance, you are giving witness to the observation which may help in the future, if further action needs to be taken. You are also giving them concrete and specific ways in which they can change and improve their performance.

Giving faculty a false sense of success will not lead to becoming a better or more effective teacher. When you give this negative feedback, try to state the observations and data objectively and without bias. When possible, add areas of success they can build upon and suggestions for growth. Together, you can develop an action plan with concrete steps for the faculty member to improve.

On the other hand, you likely have super-star teachers who are, by all accounts, excellent at their practice. Meaningful feedback is just as important to these teachers. While they may rate highly in every category on the observation instrument or rubric, the kindest approach is to help them continually grow professionally. Try to notice ways or areas they can improve in meaningful ways. During the post-observation conversations, discuss where they would like to improve and advance professionally. This communicates to them that you are genuine in your care for their growth.

Most of your faculty will fall somewhere between these two extremes. You will easily be able to identify both strengths and areas for growth in their professional practice. As you communicate with them, transformational kindness dictates that you build upon strengths and work together to develop plans to address areas of weakness. Each faculty member should leave a feedback session feeling empowered to grow as a professional.

School Policies

> At my youngest child's middle school, there has been an issue with the students getting to their classes on time. The administration has responded by implementing new consequences for tardiness: after five tardies, the student will be placed in in-school suspension, and after eight, the student will have out-of-school suspension. Now, keep in mind, owing to inconsistencies in how teachers record attendance, there are few consequences for skipping a class entirely. Therefore, a smart middle schooler will skip class rather than risk a suspension. Even without that caveat, does it make logical sense to prevent students from missing class by having them miss even more class?

Likely, the student code of conduct and contract for teachers are developed by someone higher up in the hierarchy (e.g., school board, superintendent's office, or head of schools). However, you also likely have some degree of latitude in how rules are enforced and specific policies at your school. If you are a district- or state-level administrator with more power to develop policies that inform how schools function, your responsibility for the equity and implications of these policies is even greater.

While policies help keep schools safe, orderly, and efficient, they have also been used to systematically exclude and disenfranchise groups of students, families, and faculty (Riddle & Sinclair, 2019). So, how do we, as school leaders, develop school policies that demonstrate kindness? For every school policy, we must ask ourselves four key questions:

1. What is the purpose?
2. Who does it help?
3. Who does it harm?
4. Is it kind?

What Is the Purpose?

The first step in considering a policy is to ask why it exists. Often, we put a rule in place because we have always done things that way or it is a relic of bygone days. Once upon a time, wearing a hat indoors was a huge breech of etiquette, but is that still the case in today's society? What purpose does a "no hat" policy serve in your school?

My child's middle school recently implemented a "no hoodies" policy. There are children at the school who have experienced sexual and gender-related trauma, and wearing a hoodie provides comfort, allowing them to hide parts of them that they are not yet comfortable showing the world. Forcing these children to expose themselves feels violating and retraumatizing to them. The first question, one that the administration could not adequately answer, is the purpose that the "no hoodies" policy serves.

Who Does It Help?

When considering a policy, ask yourself: what group benefits from the rule? Is there a group that is privileged by it? If you cannot identify who the policy is benefitting, then consider eliminating the policy. You may also consider whether the policy benefits a more privileged group over a more marginalized group and whether the disparity is worth the benefits of the policy.

For example, enforcing a "no running" policy in the school hallways benefits all students in the school. This keeps students safe from accidents. It also benefits teachers and staff by keeping them safe from wayward children who might run into them as they race down the hallways. It is not likely to privilege one group of students over another.

On the other hand, a policy that allows the football players to move to the front of the cafeteria line on game days benefits the football players. These students tend to be male, popular, and athletic. By giving them additional privileges through this policy, a school would be increasing the disparity between the football players and the less athletic students.

Who Does It Hurt?

Next, consider who is hurt by a policy, particularly any unintended consequences. It is all too easy for us, as administrators and school leaders, to create rules without thinking through the effects on faculty, staff, and students, particularly our most vulnerable populations or those from groups that are different from our own.

For example, if a school limits restroom breaks during instructional periods, it will certainly cut down on students skipping class to meet up in the hallways. But what about the students with diabetes or other medical conditions that necessitate more frequent restroom breaks? What about the basic needs of all human beings to relieve themselves after eating or drinking? Could limiting access to the restroom cause some students to limit their water intake and thus become dehydrated? This policy has many negative health effects, including a disregard for basic human dignity to regulate bodily functions.

Is It Kind?

Finally, asking yourself whether a policy is kind is the last step to considering a policy. Ultimately, any policy in place should have a positive impact on the school community. Does this policy build community, make students and faculty feel welcome, set appropriate boundaries, or create a safe and secure learning environment? Policies that help structure the environment for student success are kind.

School rules and policies that enforce consequences for physical assault, verbal insults, and threatening behaviors help create a safe and secure environment. Developing consequences for negative behaviors that help the offender cope with aggression in healthy ways and set them up for success is also kind and reflects a commitment to the entire school community. Providing teachers with the tools to effectively manage their classrooms is kind, helping to de-escalate conflicts and bring communities together.

Special Cases

Imagine the horror of opening up the *US News & World Report* or the *Washington Post* to find your school making

> the headlines for an ill-advised school policy. Perhaps you did not anticipate the unintended consequences of the policy. Perhaps the diverse backgrounds of the students at your school were impacted in ways that you had not foreseen. In any case, this is not a scenario that you want to live through.

Given these four essential questions regarding school policies, I am now going to take some time to consider four specific school policies and reflect on how they can be viewed through a lens of kindness. As a school leader, you may have varying degrees of influence to effect change in these areas, but it is my hope that this perspective gives you pause and helps frame some issues in a new light.

Dress Codes

> The first day of their sophomore year of high school, my oldest child came to school wearing the cutest romper. I celebrated with them, taking pictures before they left the house and hopeful for a school year filled with success and happy memories. Imagine my surprise to get a phone call just an hour later, to find out that as my child walked into the school on their first day, the school administrator pulled them into the office and issued a dress code violation. Instead of welcoming this child to a new school year, the child was made to feel ashamed of their body and as an outsider to the school. Worse, instead of attending the first classes of the day, they had to wait in the office until I could come and bring a change of clothing. So much for a great start to the school year.

Dress codes and policies around clothing worn in schools have made national news in recent years, detailing ways in which populations of students (e.g., female, students of color, and other marginalized groups) are targeted and ostracized by school leaders. Although national statistics on gender and racial disparities in dress code enforcement are difficult to come by, a large county in Florida found that over 80 percent of the dress code violations were against female students (Shields, 2021).

In Gonzalez, Texas, students (most of them female students) were made to wear prison jumpsuits when they violated school dress codes or they would be suspended (Tomaszewski, 2011). In my district, a sign at a high school indicated that "good girls" would wear more modest clothing to the prom and that immodest girls would not be allowed to enter the school event. This flier, posted by school administration, led to a viral hashtag (#SPCGoodGirl) and international press (BBC, 2017). In 2019, a Black wrestler had his locks shaved off during a New Jersey high school meet or he would have had to forfeit the match (Stubbs, 2019). Another Black student was banned from attending graduation at his Texas high school because of his natural hair, styled in locks (Cox, 2020).

Policies against "unprofessional" hairstyles that specifically ban natural hairstyles for students of color have been used to target this marginalized population. Similarly, it is no secret that dress codes about clothing are disproportionately enforced on female bodies (e.g., skirt/short length, bare midriffs, and sleeve width on tank tops). When the consequences for these violations remove students from class, the result is countless hours of lost instructional time for groups of students. Additionally, it takes already marginalized groups and disenfranchises them from school further.

Consider the alternative: what if we welcomed students to our community as they come to us? As children develop, clothing becomes an expression of their sense of self. What if schools celebrated, rather than regulated, this self-expression? Might we have more students attend school? Might some feel more welcome and a greater sense of belonging to our community? Could we increase the instructional time for our most vulnerable students?

Of course, depending on your community, you may also need to implement some commonsense regulations. Closed toe shoes might be necessary for safety, especially in a chemistry lab or physical education class. Clothing with offensive or hateful imagery or language may need to be monitored and restricted for the building of community amongst students.

Ultimately, with most restrictive dress code policies, I have yet to hear a compelling argument to answer the questions "What is the purpose?" and "Who does it help?" and I find too many groups that it harms. Dress codes do not make our communities kinder places in which to exist.

Tardies and Attendance

> My mother was a teacher in the early 1970s, just as many schools in Texas were (finally) being integrated. In the junior high school where she had one of her first teaching positions, there was quite a bit of concern over racial violence in the recently integrated school. The school hired a hall monitor to help add extra security for the students and faculty. Rather than employing a security officer or a menacing figure, the school found an older Black grandmother. She stood at the main hallway each day, greeting each child, asking about their families, and inquiring about their days. Since she was familiar with the community and knew each of the students, she was able to monitor the halls effectively. She knew where everyone was supposed to be and easily identified anyone who did not belong. The students were kept safe and accountable for being where they needed to be, but, more importantly, they felt safe and secure. If a security officer had been there to intimidate students into obedience, it very likely would have increased the tension of the school.

Think back to the vignette earlier in this chapter about suspending students after five tardies or my other child's school in which students who were even 2 seconds late to class had to go all the way to the front office for a tardy slip, a process that could take up to 15 minutes. Similarly, every school I have ever encountered puts a premium on perfect attendance, with large awards, ceremonies, and recognition for students who make this achievement.

With a bit of consideration, the logic of these policies seems absurd. The penalty for missing a bit of class is to miss even more class?! Again, what if we had the opposite reaction to tardiness. What if when a student arrived late to class, we welcomed them in and asked with concern why they were late? Perhaps we would discover a systemic problem that is causing them to be late—are they walking from the far side of campus? Do they have trouble opening their locker? Is the math teacher keeping their class after the bell? Maybe they are socializing in the hallways for too long and your concern will help them remember to move along.

When I taught in a Title 1 school of primarily low-income elementary school children, many of our students arrived to school late. I even had a student who did not come to my art class for an entire marking period, because their mother was over an hour late every Friday morning for 6 weeks. It would make no sense to penalize the students for their families being unable to get them to school on time. Rather, it took family conferences to develop solutions that would work for each individual circumstance. The key to solving the tardiness is to address the underlying problem with a solution-focused mindset. The ultimate goal should be for students to participate in as much instructional time as possible.

Recall the school's tardy policy from the beginning of this chapter. The stated purpose of this policy was to increase safety. The tardy students were congregating in hallways to engage in fighting and acts of violence, in areas that were not well supervised, as the teachers were in classrooms teaching their classes. Utilizing the paraprofessional and administrative staff to monitor the hallways shortly after the bell rings and encouraging students to go to their classes would be much more effective ways to keep the students safe.

As far as attendance goes, while we all agree that coming to school is important for academic gains, perfect attendance should not necessarily be the goal. This approach privileges able-bodied students over those with medical needs that necessitate doctor's appointments or sick days. For students from families that are struggling financially, even arriving at school each day might be a challenge. Students and families coping with mental health concerns also are at a disadvantage when there is undue pressure for perfect attendance.

Attending school is something that is largely out of the control of the student. Until the child reaches the age at which they can drive (assuming the family has the means to afford a car), families are responsible for transportation, whether that is driving them to school, sending the child to the bus stop, or walking to the school. Getting sick or having an injury is largely out of the control of the student as well.

After experiencing the global pandemic and spread of COVID-19, we are all the more cognizant of germs and contagion. To keep our schools safe, we should do the opposite. We should encourage students and faculty to stay home when they are sick and provide generous support to help them catch up when they return. When schools pivot and change this mindset, we honor the value of our entire community's health and well-being.

Along these lines, it is also important to recognize that mental health is as important as physical health. When students suffer from anxiety, depression, or other disorders, they can be just as debilitated as those with other serious and chronic diagnoses. These conditions are on the rise among adolescents and children; both depression and suicidal thoughts rose 40% from 2009 to 2019 (CDC, 2019). As a school leader, consider how your policies might support students with mental health concerns.

Zero-Tolerance Policies

> One day last year, my child came home from their middle school visibly upset. When I inquired about what was wrong, they told me about the new school policy. Now anyone who is involved in a fight, no matter who instigated it, would be suspended. No tolerance for fighting. Now, my child has never been involved in physical violence, nor do they have any intention of being in a fight. But they were terrified that another student would push them, hit them, or otherwise assault them—and then they would be suspended along with the perpetrator! What struck me

> about the conversation is that my child was not particularly afraid of the other students but was terrified of the administration and getting in trouble.

Zero-tolerance policies always strike me as the type of policy that looks better on paper than in practice. Sure, who could argue with a policy that has no tolerance for guns, illegal drugs, or assault? But when we consider these policies through the lens of kindness, we might realize that they take away the ability of school leaders to consider the humanity of each student. The only factor in the decision is the crime or offense, not the human being or personal circumstances around it.

Certainly, most zero-tolerance policies are designed to create a safer school environment. And strong consequences for members of a community that violate that sense of safety are warranted. I do not want a student who brings a gun to school with the intention of violence to continue to threaten the safety of my school community. However, as in most of life, most situations are more nuanced.

Consider the high school junior who was suspended from school after leaving his hunting rifle in the backseat of his truck after a deer hunting trip. He had no intention of bringing the gun into the building, and the gun was discovered only when the police used their K-9 unit to search the parking lot during a security check (Acosta, 2010).

Consider the kindergartener who brought what they thought was lemonade to share with their friends at school. When it turned out that the drink contained 10% alcohol as a pre-mixed cocktail, the child faced serious charges and possible suspension (Woods & Carr, 2022).

Consider that students with special needs are more likely to be bullied by classmates, and over half of autistic students with have been provoked to the point of fighting back (Walton, 2012), which could result in suspensions and harsh disciplinary actions. Or maybe it is a high school freshman, who, afraid of gun violence in his neighborhood, hides a handgun in his backpack for his walk to and from school. Perhaps it is the fifth grader who brings some of her dad's medicine to show off to her friends at school and it turns out to be a controlled substance.

In each of these cases, a zero-tolerance policy would dictate expulsion or suspension—consequences that could drastically change the life outcomes for these children. With kindness and a full understanding of the context and circumstances, a school leader could decide on a more appropriate consequence and offer support and solutions for the students involved. In all cases, it is important that the school leadership retain the ability to use their humanity and good judgment to make compassionate decisions regarding serious behavioral incidents.

Involvement of Law Enforcement

> In my teacher preparation program, we have a focus on preparing our students to work in urban schools. During a site visit to one of our partner schools, while the children were playing at recess on the playground that shares space with a community park, an armed man ran across the public park. He was followed shortly by several police cars with sirens and uniformed officers chasing him on foot. The first-grade children were, understandably, terrified. But my teacher candidates were baffled to learn that the children were more scared of the police than the armed man. Being part of a community that has been historically and currently the target of police brutality, the children were naturally distrustful of law enforcement—a concept that was unfamiliar to our mostly upper-middle-class White teacher candidates.

Increasingly, law enforcement, police, or uniformed security guards have been involved in the everyday life at schools (Curran, 2020), despite evidence that the presence of officers has little effect on school safety (King & Bracy, 2019). The negative and unintended effects of school resource officers or law enforcement in schools, however, are serious and consequential. Paradoxically, they have a negative impact on school climate, perhaps making many students and families feel less safe (King & Bracy, 2019).

Additionally, they have been linked to the school-to-prison pipeline, in which marginalized and at-risk youth have their first encounter with the juvenile justice system through incidents at school (Heise & Nance, 2021). While ostensibly school resource officers, police presence, and law enforcement are there as part of plans to increase school safety, they often do not have the desired effect. The National Association of School Psychologists has created a comprehensive resource to help inform school leaders about school safety and mental health (NASP, 2018), and a list of additional resources can be found in the Resources section at the end of this book.

The expression "if you are holding a hammer, everything looks like a nail" rings true in this scenario. When a school has a school resource officer or safety officer, behaviors that would traditionally be handled by a teacher, counselor, or administrator are turned over to law enforcement. These officers, while undoubtedly well trained for their duties in the police force, typically have little to no specialized training in child development, de-escalating conflicts, or mental health (Bolger et al., 2018).

We are now seeing reports of elementary school children as young as five years old being detained, arrested, and handcuffed for having disrupted class (Levenson & Burnside, 2020), sent a text message (Robinson, 2022), left school (Lenthang, 2021), or kicked a classmate in kindergarten (Chiu, 2019). This first involvement with the criminal justice system is traumatic for these very young children, for many of whom the police do not even have handcuffs small enough for their tiny wrists.

Arrests that happen to older children, like the middle school student in Old Saybrook, Connecticut (Sobol, 2022), can start a cycle of arrests and lead to a path of disenfranchisement (Novak, 2019). Instead of criminalizing behaviors in schools, we, as school leaders, should be guiding students into developing skills to successfully deal with conflict through restorative justice and supporting teachers in effectively managing behavioral disruptions in their classrooms (NASP, 2018).

When we consider the relationship that many students, families, and communities have with law enforcement, it might also give us pause to reconsider having a strong police presence in our schools. What message might we unintentionally be sending to our students and community, particularly to those groups that have been historically harmed by systems of law enforcement? Do the police officers on campus make everyone in the school feel safer? Research suggests that for students (particularly students of color), the presence of a school resource officer tends to make them feel less safe (Mowen & Freng, 2019).

If your school does have a school resource officer, as is required by Florida state law (Marjory Stoneman Douglas High School Public Safety Act, 2018) and increasingly ubiquitous across the country, carefully consider how you can best utilize this resource for your community. Are there opportunities to include the officer in school-wide professional learning or community events? Are there ways to build bridges of trust and communication to the community? Can you establish clear boundaries to protect students from needless interactions with the criminal justice system and rely on restorative justice measures instead? This could be an opportunity to make a great deal of change in your wider community, if approached with radical and transformational kindness.

Overall, being a school leader comes with a great deal of responsibility. You must set the tone and build the foundation for the community of kindness at your school. However, by adopting these principles and the lens of kindness, you can also see your work transform your educational world. Your community can be a place where you and your faculty, staff, students, and families can thrive and all members can lift each other up. You may not be perfect, but when you are kind, your community will flourish.

4

Kindness Towards Students

The skirt was dark yellow and white checked gingham. The short-sleeved blouse was light yellow and white gingham with a slightly smaller check. Close but not a match. On the blouse, she always wore a small pin made from a piece of brown striped petrified wood. I marveled at the idea of wood petrifying and that by some magic my fifth-grade teacher would have a specimen of petrified wood to wear.

Mrs. Leonard, in fact, was magic. After four years of teachers who seemed to tolerate their students, I was assigned to one who loved teaching. We weren't students; we were people.

My first-grade teacher, Mrs. Quy, was fired at the end of the fall term. Mrs. Humphrey took over, but I really couldn't tell the difference much. I spent most of the year in the hall by myself anyway. Second grade's Mrs. Housewright didn't know how to control me and kept consulting Mom, who taught next door. My third-grade teacher, Mrs. Harrison, didn't bother to notice that my desk mate and I had an ongoing war, resulting in daily scratches on our arms. I only remember Mrs. Thomas standing straight and proper in front of the dark blackboard, writing in chalk. Nothing shines brightly from that year.

Mrs. Leonard taught us fractions. You'd think that would be boring, but it wasn't. There was a bright red and white poster showing a pie chart on the wall. I understood.

Each week, we colored in one state of the USA on a mimeographed piece of paper and learned its capital and its major exports. The best drawings were tacked to the bulletin boards. Reds, blues, greens, and yellows highlighting states. We learned to shade the edges darker than the center and keep our crayon lines smooth.

To better convey a sense of the early days of our country, she had all of us learn how to braid a rug. Even the boys. Colored pieces of leftover fabric were braided and sewn into oblong mats. We were allowed to work anywhere we wanted in the room. We scattered, rearranged ourselves, and found new friends in the relaxed mess. Bright fabric scraps drifted around us as we braided and sewed.

Everyone was equal in Mrs. Leonard's room. She encouraged one boy—who attended only that one year, who was behind most of the class academically, and I suspect was from a migrant working family—to show off his ability to do calligraphy. Looking back, I think she extended some recess time so he could produce drawings for those of us who asked. The girl who lived in a dilapidated brown house on the corner of the school lot had yellow-green teeth and old clothes. She was treated with respect and not ignored. I know that it was the first year that this girl was really part of a classroom. I KNEW that if Mrs. Leonard accepted them that she accepted me, too.

DOI: 10.4324/9781003250739-4

For the first years at Davey Crockett Elementary School, my classrooms faced the inner courtyard, grey and barren, with hard packed down dirt. The rooms were dark. In fifth grade, the wall of windows, waist-high to the ceiling, faced the street. Green bushes, trees, and grass stood against the small cottages, each a different hue, across the street. The Texas sky was blue.

She took us to the school's library, and I began to read. I read all the red biographies for the fifth graders, but the librarian wouldn't let me read the orange-bound ones meant for sixth graders. I should have asked Mrs. Leonard. I bet she would have figured out a way for me to move from red to orange.

At the end of the year, Mrs. Leonard let me have all the leftover construction paper scraps. Her kindness, her teaching, her care was all mixed in with that colorful bag I took home for the summer.

I went from classrooms of properness, of straightness, of rigidity, where we all sat in even rows, to a classroom where the desks moved and the teacher fostered happiness. Fun wasn't restricted to recess. Learning was interwoven into experiences.

It was like going from black and white to color.

(A special thank-you to my mother, Chris Fulmer, for contributing this vignette from her childhood in the 1950s in Abilene, Texas.)

I hope that we all have a story like this one from my mother, about a teacher who was kind, a teacher who built relationships and changed the course of our lives. This is the reason that many of us entered the field of education and what most of us strive to be for our students. In this chapter, we will explore the ways in which we can demonstrate this transformational kindness in our classrooms and towards our students.

In this age of accountability and competition for resources in education (Kim, 2018), many school systems have lost the compassion and kindness towards the very people who they are designed to serve—the students. Our students are the most vulnerable, and also the most resilient, members of our educational community, and the ones with the least agency to choose their level of participation within it.

When I teach my pre-service teacher candidates, they speak of their love for children, excitement to make a difference in lives, and compassion for those who struggle. When I visit schools, I see teachers short of time, facing pressures of test scores, paperwork, scripted curriculum, and shortages of personnel. Working within a system that often sees students as numbers rather than human beings and facing unmeasurable amounts of daily stress, you can easily lose the spark that originally brought you into teaching.

In March of 2020, the entire world shifted, and teachers were asked to take on the added responsibilities of teaching during an international crisis. Switching entire pedagogies to virtual or hybrid instruction in a matter of weeks or attempting to get children to stay socially distanced, wear masks all day, and continually wash their hands—teachers made Herculean efforts! And as the pandemic wore on, the extended trauma, exhaustion, and unwavering expectations have had a negative effect on both students and teachers. Without the face-to-face interactions, many students became disengaged. As students became disengaged, many teachers became less understanding of missing work and less creative in finding ways to support learners. Everyone was exhausted.

Of course, I also saw extraordinary examples of teachers going out of their way and beyond their assigned duties to connect with students. I saw schools go to great lengths to innovate and keep students engaged. We saw graduation car parades, meals delivered by school buses, and teachers tutoring students from the backs of pick-up trucks. But the overwhelming fatigue felt by so many members of our school community, particularly in the aftermath of the pandemic in the 2021–2022 school year, underscores the underlying problems that were already present.

Until we, as teachers and as educational communities, can see each and every student who walks into our classroom and school as valuable human beings worthy of respect and educational opportunities, we will not be able to change our schools with transformational kindness. This is a lofty goal, one that is not easily accomplished. We will struggle with that student who knows how to push all of our buttons, that student who is apathetic and has not submitted a single assignment all semester, or that student who cannot seem to stop socializing during every single lesson you teach.

But even through those struggles, we can see the humanity in each child and view each interaction through the lens of transformational kindness. The child who is pushing your buttons? Maybe they need positive attention. Could we frame their comments as witty and clever rather than rude and disrespectful? The child who is apathetic? Maybe they are experiencing trauma or have an undiagnosed learning disability. Could we frame their behavior as an opportunity for us as a teacher to engage the child in meaningful work? The child who will not stop talking? Maybe they need direction on how to better direct their social energies. Could we frame their behavior as a positive trait? Maybe this child will be a future politician or top sales associate?

In the last chapter of the book, I will address kindness to self and how you can protect yourself from educator burnout. So, as we care for each of the humans in our classroom, we must also remember that we are also part of the community that needs kindness.

In this chapter, I will address building this community of kindness towards students from the perspective of teachers. This includes classroom management, pedagogy, curriculum, and assessment. Shifting perspectives from accountability to transformational kindness has the potential to meaningfully impact your career, your students, and the environment around you.

Building Relationships

> My youngest child, like many middle-school-aged children, struggled to find their way through the social milieu of adolescence. This was made particularly difficult because of the COVID-19 pandemic and being remote for most of their sixth-grade year. Then in seventh grade, they learned that the beloved sixth-grade English/language arts teacher would be moving up to seventh grade to teach this cohort again. Thank goodness for Ms. Isabella Araujo—at least my child would have one familiar face when they returned for the school year. Then I found myself driving my child to school an hour early 2 days a week, so that they could be part of the gaming club at school, advised by none other than Ms. Araujo. This kind woman not only arrived at school early, giving up her precious planning time, to be with these squirrelly middle schoolers on Mondays and Wednesdays, but (as I found out) she was actually participating in their *Dungeons & Dragons* campaign! As they continued the play

over winter and spring breaks, I saw this adult make a space for these children, creating an environment in which they could be themselves, feel accepted, and know that they were valued.

The foundation of a kind community is made up of relationships. Studies have shown what experienced teachers have long known that students achieve more when they have a good relationship with their teacher (e.g., Chamizo-Nieto et al., 2021). And while school systems focus on building their punitive measures for teachers, students, and schools that do not meet benchmarks on standardized assessments, fewer are invested in building relationships with students.

Renowned developmental psychologist Abraham Maslow (1943) discussed a hierarchy of needs, acknowledging that people need love and belonging before they can pursue higher goals, such as education and learning. Of course, some students are resilient and are able to persist in education despite all odds and adversity, and we can name success stories of people who overcame a lack of basic needs (love, acceptance, safety, etc.) to achieve educational goals. But how many more are lost because of a system that lacks care for individuals? And how many more would achieve greater success in life if they knew that the adults at school were personally invested in their success?

Other studies of student success and at-risk students demonstrate that if a child has at least one trusted adult at school, their risk of dropping out, failure, suicide, and substance abuse is greatly reduced (e.g., Whitehead et al., 2019). And we, as educators, have the awesome opportunity (and responsibility) to develop these communities and relationships with students.

The three parts of a building relationship with students are:

1. **Unconditional positive regard**: Respect for the humanity of all people in the classroom
2. **Mutual trust**: Initially believing best intentions and giving opportunities for everyone to show their best
3. **Take interest**: Know each person as an individual, finding common ground and showing up for them.

Unconditional Positive Regard

> How often do we refer to students as a "Level 3" or an "A student" rather than as a whole person, with likes and dislikes, strengths and interests outside of their academic performance? How often do we see beyond the problem behaviors to the heart and soul of the child?

In building a relationship with students, as with all groups, a good starting point is unconditional positive regard for them as human beings. Seeing students not as grades on a report card, numbers on a spreadsheet, or as underlings—but as fellow humans, worthy of respect, will instantly change how you interact with them.

Each child in your classroom has humanity, and as they move through our institutions, it can be all too easy to lose track of this quality. We can convey our unconditional positive regard through simple things, such as our tone of voice or our facial expressions. A quick smile and a kind tone can change the mood and recognize the humanity of a child. Classroom practices that acknowledge basic human needs, such as ready access to the restroom, snacks and drinks, and interaction with peers, also help to convey our regard for students.

Mutual Trust

On the other hand, when adults approach classrooms with suspicion, the students tend to live up to those expectations. When a teacher says, "You have to earn my respect," the burden of developing the relationship is on the novice, a child who has about as much experience with this as they do with electrical sockets.

However, when adults begin relationships with the expectation of mutual trust, believing that the students have good intentions, students tend to rise to these standards as well. Giving opportunities for students to show you their best will go a long way to developing trust. This is particularly true when you can scaffold their independence and foster self-regulatory skills.

Depending on the developmental stage of your students, the opportunities to demonstrate trust may vary in scope. Perhaps the opportunity presents itself when you need to step outside the classroom for a moment to ask the teacher across the hallway a question. Or maybe it is five minutes of free time at the end of a lecture, selecting their own partners for group work or self-grading their quizzes. As you set expectations and trust grows, you will find that you have more freedom in the classroom and that everyone enjoys being at school more.

Of course, there will be times when individual students, or whole groups of students, break your trust. This is the true test of the tenuous relationship that you are building with your students. Are you going to be the adult who dumps them after one mistake (or several mistakes)? Or are you going to be the adult whom they can trust to stand by them through difficult times? Acknowledging your own feelings here is critical. It may have hurt you deeply, you may be very angry or upset. However, it is imperative that you remain in control of your emotions in front of your students. You can let them know how their actions affected your relationship and caused harm, but you also need to allow them redemption and show them their value to you.

I will discuss logical consequences and correcting behavior in the Classroom Management section later in this chapter, but for now, let's concentrate on building trust with students. After you address the specific behaviors with students, it is important to begin to re-establish trust. You may need to start with small goals, but giving students chances to demonstrate that you can trust them is important to rebuilding the relationship.

Take Interest

When my oldest child was a freshman, making the difficult adjustment to a new school and still unsure of themselves, they had a small part in a community production of *Bye Bye Birdie*. Their high school theater teacher, Mr. Jeff Grove, made the time to come and see them in the show, congratulating them on the show after curtain call and complimenting the performance. This made all the difference in their confidence as an actor, their place in the school community, and their sense of belonging in the theater program.

Finally, building a relationship involves taking interest in the other person. For students, this means knowing about their worlds. Maybe you read the latest book series that your students are obsessing over or you catch the movie that they lined up to see at midnight. It could be as simple as asking about their soccer game or if their favorite band has any shows coming up. The key component is knowing your students as individuals and caring about their interests.

I think back to Mr. Grove: the time that he took to appreciate my child's theater performance made a difference in our lives. Of course, teachers do not have the time or energy to attend every game, performance, or competition for every one of their students. But, when that effort is made, the effect is meaningful and long-lasting. It is important and time well spent when it is possible.

Overall, the foundation of transformational kindness in the classroom consists of relationships. Building a relationship is based on unconditional positive regard, mutual trust, and taking interest. The energy that you put into developing this relational community will pay dividends in the increased joy and achievement inside and outside of your classroom.

Classroom Management

During my oldest child's first week of the seventh grade, I got the standardized test scores back from the previous year. When I saw a significant drop in the mathematics score, I immediately made an appointment to speak with her current math teacher, Mr. Matt Peterson. As I entered the room, he reassured me that my child's math score would be fine and that he had already identified their

> areas of strength in algebra. But what struck me most from the conversation was the comment he made at the end of the meeting. He told me that my child had made plenty of friends in the class and that on the next day, he would be changing the seating arrangement so that my child could be less distracted by the social interactions. This teacher had known my child for only a week and had already identified their strengths and recognized that sitting next to their friends was going to be detrimental to their education. And, best of all, Mr. Peterson framed this not as a failure on my child's part but as a positive quality and one that he would adapt his classroom to accommodate. We both left the conference feeling great about the upcoming year.

As we think about framing our classrooms around cultures of kindness, classroom management or expectations for student behavior may be among the first things that we consider. When the teacher builds a strong and healthy classroom community with meaningful relationships among and with students, as Mr. Peterson did, many issues of classroom management will resolve themselves. When students feel safe and cared for in a community of learning, they are less likely to act out and disrupt that community.

Communities of Learning

Leaning on the research of Barbara Rogoff and her theories regarding sociocultural learning (Rogoff et al., 2001), we all naturally learn in a community from our skilled elders and our peers through both tacit and direct instruction. From this perspective, we can think of our classroom as a microculture in which we develop norms of behavior through our actions as the leader or guide.

Indirectly, through modeling respect for every student (remember Ms. Leonard?), a teacher can convey the unconditional positive regard that all students should have for each other. This modeling can also apply to the tone of your voice, keeping the room tidy, and other pro-social behaviors.

For other circumstances, as you work to establish these behavioral norms, more explicit and direct instruction is needed. Bringing the idea of community into these moments can be helpful. For example, "The students in Dr. Wilson's class push in their chairs when we go to lunch." Or the community could be tied to a school-wide initiative, such as "Central High Eagles stop and listen to each other during class discussions."

By working to create unity in your classroom among your students and yourself and to build a community of learners, you can foster an environment that is conducive to pro-social behaviors and kindness for all students. This community of learning becomes a place where students are learning, from you and from their peers, both academic and social lessons through direct and indirect instructional lessons.

Expectations

> My youngest child had the great privilege of having the same amazing co-teachers in second and third grade and one of the teachers returned for fifth grade. Over time, this group of students became like a family, knowing each other's quirks, interests, and habits. From the early years, what I remember most about the classroom were the expectations that Ms. Laurie Justo and Ms. Carrie McLeod held for the children. During independent work time, the students had choices about where to sit in the room (bean bag chairs, pillows on the floor, worktables, and individual desks), and they did not have to ask to go to the restroom; they just needed to quietly leave the bottle of hand sanitizer on their desk to signal where they had gone. The students all had jobs each week in the classroom, and at the end of each day, they were organized to sweep the floors, put the chairs away, and reset the whiteboard. During the two years that the students had Ms. McLeod and Ms. Justo and the additional year with Ms. McLeod, the academic levels of the students excelled, but more importantly, their social skills and confidence

> grew. Children who were alienated and distant going into second grade graduated from elementary school with a close group of friends and their heads held high. Each child was celebrated for their strengths, and because of the high expectations and support of their teachers, they achieved well above the grade-level standards.

As you develop your community of learners in your classroom, the tone and climate must be carefully nurtured. You are responsible for creating a warm and safe ecosystem—much like an egg in an incubator—to welcome your students into the world and away from their parents. You can do this by having clear and high expectations for student behavior and emphasizing transformational kindness towards others, self, and the classroom. By quickly redirecting students who violate the culture of kindness, you can maintain the healthy environment to nurture learners in your classroom. It is important that you, as the guide and leader in the community, set the expectation that all members act with kindness.

Addressing Misbehaviors

> In my tenth-grade chemistry class, we were doing a lab about light spectrometry. This involved lighting various materials on fire with the Bunsen burners and measuring the patterns of the light waves through a spectroscope. One group of boys in my class decided to extend this experiment to other objects in the classroom, including mechanical pencils, notebooks, and other school supplies. Our chemistry teacher, Ms. Kimberly Kass, did not overreact to the situation. Instead, she calmly told the boys that they had lost their privileges to use the lab equipment for the rest of the semester and assigned them alternate assignments in lieu of lab projects. She did not berate the students, but she also reassured the rest of the class that there were strong consequences for their actions and that we would be kept safe during future lab assignments from wayward fire hazards. I distinctly remember that

later in the semester, Ms. Kass continued to treat the boys with respect, laughing and joking with them during class discussions, even though they were still not allowed near the Bunsen burners!

Of course, as you set high expectations for transformational kindness, there will be times at which members of the community do not live up to them. During these times, it is vital that we also keep kindness at the focus of our actions. This is the opportunity to demonstrate to our entire classroom community that they can trust us.

For the student who violated the community expectations, you must balance having empathy for their circumstances, motivation, and personhood and having high expectations for their actions. It is transformational kindness to guide them to learning how to navigate the world in a way that develops relationships with people and fosters respect for community. If we fail to address these behaviors, then we are missing the opportunity to guide the child to better choices. Worse, we are tacitly communicating to the student, and the rest of the community, that the behavior is acceptable. Imagine if the boys had suffered no consequences for melting mechanical pencils during the chemistry lab! Even if they had been naturally curious and the fires were an innocent lack of judgment, it was important that they (and the rest of the class) know that there are penalties for not following lab safety. (Thank you, Ms. Kass!)

On the other hand, when addressing behavior, those in authority too often forget the humanity of the other person in the conflict. Harsh punishments, "one size fits all" behavior plans, and humiliation techniques used by teachers defeat the objective of building community and developing pro-social behaviors. In fact, these techniques serve to further alienate the child rather than bring them closer to the group and established community practices. The goal of addressing negative behaviors should be to redirect, set expectations, and resolve the conflict while ensuring that the student is a valued member of your community.

As you address these conflicts, you may find it helpful to work with the student to delineate the motivation of the behavior.

Once you know the origin of the conflict or actions, you can work as a team with the student to find a solution to prevent future missteps. Remember: it is not you against the student but you and the student against the problem.

Resolving Conflicts and Solving Problems

I know a kindergarten boy who came home every day from school with a behavior note from his teacher: for not listening, not following directions, not staying on task, getting out of his seat, or playing during instructional time. As the school year wore on, this child, once happy to go to school, became more withdrawn. But the notes continued. The teacher grew more and more frustrated, adding stronger punishments for misbehavior and greater rewards for good behavior. By Thanksgiving, the child was at a loss, unable to please his teacher and control his actions. He asked his parents, "Am I going to grow up to be a bad guy?" As he was more and more unable to meet the demands of his teacher, he began to have meltdowns at school. Crying in frustration and unable to regulate his behavior, the boy was clearly unhappy. The teacher, in her attempts to correct his behavior, became increasingly punitive and isolated the child more and more from the classroom community. As the school year neared spring, the teacher, the child, and the parents were just counting the days until summer and a chance to start again in first grade. No one was enjoying the kindergarten year.

Fast-forward to late elementary school: with a nurturing and kind teacher, a parent who had the resources to seek outside educational evaluations, and a child who was willing to reengage in school, the boy was officially diagnosed with attention-deficit/hyperactivity disorder (ADHD) (inattentive type) and social anxiety disorder. These likely contributed to the many issues in kindergarten and explain why stronger punishments and the offer of greater rewards, in the absence

> of supportive structures, did not change his behaviors and led to negative outcomes. Luckily, this story has a happy ending, and the family and the child were able to bounce back from the very negative start to their educational journey. The same cannot be said for every child in this situation.

Unfortunately, many issues with classroom behavior (at all levels of education) are due to diagnosed and undiagnosed learning and behavioral exceptionalities such as ADHD (both hyperactive and inattentive types), anxiety, depression, dyslexia, autism spectrum disorder (ASD), oppositional defiant disorder (ODD), and the list goes on. As teachers, we are unlikely to have the expertise to identify or diagnose these disorders, but they are important to consider, particularly when a child struggles to meet expectations, despite their intentions. It is important to rely on the expertise of your school's special education department, counselors, and psychologists to identify and provide services to students who need additional support.

As a side note, do not assume that you are off the hook for undiagnosed exceptionalities if you teach secondary school. We did not realize that my own child has ADHD until their sophomore year of high school, despite my areas of expertise in education and background knowledge about the warning signs! In fact, I often have students in my undergraduate courses who receive their first diagnosis during their university years, after years of struggling through school.

Other sources of conflict may be relationships within the community, either with you or between peers. As students develop, they are learning how to navigate friendships and relationships with adults, which can cause conflicts, attempts to impress peers by acting out, or a need to socialize (even when you are trying to teach!). You can relieve some of the source of this conflict by addressing problematic behaviors away from the presence of peers. Publicly disciplining a child, embarrassing them in front of the class, or otherwise using humiliation to change behavior is likely to have a detrimental effect on not only your relationship with them but also the long-term outcomes of how the student acts in your classroom. You can often help resolve conflicts between peers or find more positive ways for students to impress their peers or times in which to socialize. However, sometimes, the assistance of school counselors or other school support staff can help when such support is available.

At other times, the conflict lays outside of your classroom community. A student who has an issue with another teacher or school personnel or family member, or is facing challenges outside of school, comes into your classroom with additional needs from your classroom community. While you cannot resolve these conflicts, you can establish your classroom as a respite from other sources of problems and as a safe and welcoming place.

Finally, the conflict may be with you. Just like any two people in the world, a teacher and a student sometimes may not be all that compatible. However, it is your job as the adult to help that student feel welcome and work to resolve the conflict—that is why we get paid the big bucks—ha ha! In all seriousness, there might be times when a conflict arises directly between you and a student. They may directly confront you, defy you, or act in ways that are hurtful towards you. As a human being, you probably feel (rightfully) angry, sad, and/or frustrated. But we must remember the power balance here: we are the figures of authority, and with that power, we must act responsibly. Therefore, it is vital to the health of our entire community that we not take our feelings out on the student. Instead, we should take the time we need to process our own emotions, remember the humanity of the student, and then work with them on a solution to the conflict.

As a side note, common sense prevails here. If the safety of you or your students is in danger, you should immediately follow your school's safety plan. Sometimes the kindest action is raising your voice, yelling, or otherwise acting out of character to get your students' attention and move them into a safe space. Additionally, no one should be subjected to verbal or emotional abuse. If you are being abused by a student, insisting on the support of your school administration and perhaps the help of your teachers' union (if available) is warranted.

Seeking Help

> Being a novice teacher in an art classroom for the first time and teaching over 800 students (kindergarten through fifth grade) each week, I was often confused about when I should refer a child's behavior to the school administration. Often overwhelmed, I remember one incident when a fourth-grader decided to paint the hallways of the school with one of the paintbrushes taken from my classroom during a restroom break! I honestly did not know where to go for help with building a nurturing classroom environment (particularly when I saw my students for only 45 minutes once a week) and how to control their sometimes (often?) out-of-control behavior. Eventually, I got the hang of it, and by the end of my time at the elementary school, I had a great relationship with my students, and there were no more painted hallways.

As a teacher, the balance of utilizing the dean of discipline, assistant principal, or administrative staff for student behavior can be difficult to navigate. Each school is different, and, of course, every administrator has their personal preferences on how behaviors should be handled. Additionally, this balance is predicated on building a strong relationship of trust with the administration.

As a rule of thumb, it is best to handle conflict within the community of your classroom rather than seek outside help. This builds trust, establishes the norms of your classroom, and allows you to build conflict resolution skills with your students. It also helps your students see you as the leader of your classroom. However, there are times in which the conflict escalates beyond what is possible to handle in your classroom.

Sometimes the behavior threatens the safety of the entire school community and must be reported to the school administration. For example, assault or the threat of assault, possession of a weapon, or controlled substance. Do not hesitate in these instances; you must act kindly to the entire community to protect their safety.

At other times, the conflict is outside of your classroom community, and you may need to go to the administration if the actions of another teacher, student, or school policy are causing conflict in your classroom. For example, if another teacher is keeping students after the bell and then they are tardy to your class, this might be a concern that needs to be brought to administration. Be sure that you can address these issues with delicacy and remember the humanity of all involved.

The most difficult issues are when you have attempted to address the behavior in your classroom and the conflict remains unresolved. Now, if I had a magic solution to this problem, I would already be retired on a beach somewhere. Unfortunately, the solution for this situation will depend completely on your context. The first step may be to seek the advice and wisdom of your colleagues and fellow teachers, possibly those who also teach the student or have taught them in the past. The best advice that I have gotten in my career has come from my co-workers, and I am sure that you have had similar experiences. The teacher community is a wonderful thing.

Depending on your relationship with your administration, you may want to meet with them to discuss the situation. They may be able to provide support, coaching, or insight. The school counselor or psychologist may also be helpful in providing support for the student or offering ways in which you could address the behaviors. Meeting with the administration separately, rather than referring the student to their offices, can be a more solution-focused approach. This conversation can lead to guidance on when it would be appropriate for the administrator to directly intervene. Ideally, you have a relationship built with the leadership at your school, and this meeting would be one that is fruitful and supportive. If this is not the case in your school community, you may be better served by handling the situation yourself or following the written guidelines and policies of your school.

A final note on seeking help. As trusted adults, teachers are sometime the confidants for students. It is our moral and ethical (and also legal!) responsibility to seek help for our students when we have any reason to suspect child abuse (physical, sexual, emotional, or neglect). Remember that it is not your job to determine whether the abuse happened, only to report your suspicions, so that an investigation can occur.

As a teacher, you are also the first line of contact with students who are at risk for suicide and self-harm. Be sure that you are familiar with the signs and symptoms of suicide and self-harm (see the Resources section). It is important that you take any suggestion or talk of suicide or self-harm seriously, even if it is framed as a joke. It is better to be cautious than to regret not acting. You are not responsible for determining whether a child is truly suicidal, only to report the concerns so that they can get help and a determination can be made.

For these reasons, you should never promise a child that you will keep their secrets or that you will not tell anyone what they tell you. You must report any information that puts children at risk for physical, mental, or emotional danger. Ask your school administrator to whom you should report these concerns if you do not already know who the members of the school crisis team are. Do not hesitate to seek help for students if you suspect they need it. Sometimes asking for help is the kindest course of action.

Classroom Expectations

> In the first elementary school where I taught, the measure of a good teacher was how quietly your students could walk down the hallway. In perfectly straight lines—one line for boys and one line for girls—with hands behind the back and mouths closed, the children were expected to follow along the straight path to their next activity. And the very best teachers had classes that were so silent in the hallways, you didn't even know they were coming! And what respect I had for those seasoned practitioners—to have that amount of control over their students... I was in awe.
>
> Then I transferred to a new school, and the atmosphere was completely different. The classes did not come to the art room in perfectly lined-up rows; they walked as a group, quietly making conversation. Perhaps the teacher would ask the class about what they saw in the hallway

> or remind them about the schedule for the rest of the day. The children were responsible for their own bodies, managing to proceed from activity to activity without the structure of strict lines. They seemed to enjoy each other's company and the respect that was given to them. It was not chaos but rather an organic movement from one area to the next, much like a group of co-workers moving from the office to the restaurant across the street for lunch. And the most well-respected teachers? They were the ones who were engaging their learners in deep conversation, developing relationships, and exploring the world around them.
>
> When I think back to these two schools, I am struck by the dichotomy of how the cultures of each school were so different. And I think about how, if I were a student, the second school would be a much more enjoyable place to spend 7 hours a day. And I wonder how difficult it would be for all teachers to adopt policies that gave students responsibility and autonomy for making choices, rather than to dictate the smallest of their movements.

As you develop your classroom environment and nurture community among your students, you must consider the specific expectations necessary for an effective and safe learning environment. When deciding on an expectation or policy, consider the following questions (addressed in more detail in Chapter 3):

1. What is the purpose?
2. Who does it help?
3. Who does it hurt?
4. Is it kind?

Too often, we, as teachers, have rules in our learning spaces because it has always been done this way or because it is convenient for the adults. When we change our orientation towards transformational kindness, we open the space to question our policies and shift to a student-centered approach for our expectations.

A rule of thumb is that the fewer restrictions on student activity, the more trust and motivation you will have from students. Of course, this is balanced by needs of safety and the ability of the students to regulate their behavior to maintain a safe and effective learning environment. However, as you allow more choice and autonomy, set fewer limitations, and practice greater acceptance, you will notice a more positive working climate.

For example, allowing students to wear hats or hoodies, eat snacks, chew gum, use purple ink pens, check their phones after their work is completed, read graphic novels (instead of chapter books), or other relatively minor freedoms pays dividends in student engagement and helping students feel a part of your community.

In the rest of this section, I will address specific classroom policies and how they may impact student learning, acceptance, and the learning environment.

Restroom Breaks

Of all the indignities faced by public school students, those around urination and defecation (not to mention menstruation for pubescent adolescents) are, in my mind, the most egregious. Have we, as a school system, stopped to consider the implications of regulating the basic bodily functions of our nation's children, human beings with needs, wants, and dignity? As the title of the popular children's book states, "Everyone Poops" (Gomi, 2020), and we as the authority figures in the classroom should not be in the business of regulating it. Nor should students be ostracized when they need to utilize the facilities by wearing ridiculous "restroom passes" such as bright orange safety vests or rewarded for not expressing their bodily functions.

Some schools have issues with students using restroom breaks for unacceptable behaviors. Yes, I am aware that some of our clever students have devised schemes to sneak in some PDA (public displays of affection) or physical altercations by carefully timing their restroom breaks with others. In these cases, the issue could be better solved by increased hallway monitoring rather than by restricting the human dignity of all students. For the first point, restrictive restroom policies harm students by stripping them of dignity, health, and bodily autonomy. And, secondly, if students have enough motivation, they will find a way to leave class, and having someone monitor the hallways will be more effective in keeping students safe.

As a former teacher of kindergarteners, I also know the frustration of children missing key instructional time because of restroom needs (or perhaps excuses to wander down the hallway and back again?). This can be solved by setting clear community expectations. Discussing the best times to use the restroom (e.g., during individual work time, group restroom breaks, and recess) and acknowledging the need for occasional "emergencies" during instructional time are the keys to success. Primary-age teachers are likely familiar with this topic, as to avoid the inevitable accidents in their classroom. (I once had a child get halfway to the restroom and then return to my classroom to vomit in the doorway because they were not sure they could make it to the restroom in time!) It would behoove secondary teachers to set similar expectations for their classrooms; quite frankly, a 5-minute passing period is unlikely to be long enough for most people to get the needed materials for class, walk across a large campus, and tend to their restroom needs. Acknowledging the humanity of each student and their autonomy to know their own bodily needs is a key component of building trust and developing a classroom through transformational kindness.

Consider that our bodies are designed to work on a schedule. That means that it is actually quite likely that a student would need to use the restroom at the same time each day (e.g., midway through your fourth-period class, 30 minutes after lunch). Many schools do not have passing periods that are long enough for restroom breaks, or students have classes that are far apart, or the restrooms are overly crowded during these times. If the repeated restroom breaks become disruptive to learning, you could consider problem-solving with the student to find a solution, or, you know, you could just let them go.

It is often difficult for young teens to navigate the proper maintenance of menstruation. As teachers, we must be particularly sensitive to these issues, allowing time to change products as necessary (and perhaps without verbal explanation). If none is readily available at your school, you may also consider keeping a supply of products available for use.

In all things, consider kindness and how your policies around restroom breaks impact the trust, autonomy, and human dignity of your classroom community.

Socializing

All human beings have a basic need to socialize and be in community. Unfortunately, sometimes students' need for socializing interferes with the learning environment. Too often, teachers combat this by forbidding all forms of communication—leading to a stand-off between students and teachers and a pretty dreary classroom environment. There are even schools, and teachers, that have banned socialization and talking during free periods, such as lunch and passing periods. Can you imagine sitting in the teachers' lounge and being forbidden from speaking to your friends and co-workers?

Of course, there are times when silence is, indeed, golden (e.g., during assessments or writing time). But the more opportunities we give students to share ideas, thoughts, and experiences with peers, the more engaged your students will be in the learning. Personally, I cannot stand professional learning workshops when I am not allowed to talk with the people at my table, giving time to discuss the ideas present and how they will apply to our own work. I need that time to process, interact, and engage with the topic.

Students also need time to socialize that is not strictly limited to curricular topics, by having some time allotted to building community through general socializing (whether through whole class meetings or small group discussions, structured or unstructured conversations). This recognizes the basic human need to be social creatures and feel part of the community. Just a simple check-in with students and sharing a challenge and celebration at the beginning of each week can help a class bond together and build community.

Public Behavior Charts

A common feature in elementary classrooms across the country are public behavior charts, in which each child's name is listed along with a symbol of their status of behavior for the day (or week). This could be a clothespin that moves up and down a chart, a pushpin that moves along a line, or an index card that flips colors. In secondary school, this could take the form of writing a student's name on the board for each infraction. Based upon the ubiquity of this concept, I personally wonder how many teachers have stopped to consider the kindness and humanity of these plans.

As an adult, I doubt that many of us would want a visual reminder of our mistakes—much less one that hung on the wall for all of our peers to see. When we consider the Family Educational Rights and Privacy Act (FERPA) and the protections that federal law provides to students for the confidentiality of their educational records, those behavior charts seem to violate the spirit, if not the letter, of the law. This public proclamation of a student's behavior can be a humiliating experience, one that brings feelings of shame and worthlessness, and can result in alienation and withdrawal from the community. Thus, it could have the opposite of the desired effect.

Additionally, behavior charts give a false sense that all violations of community expectations are equal. Talking during a quiz is very different than talking while getting ready for lunch (neither of which may be in need of correction, depending on the context). Furthermore, the behavioral goals for every student may be very different. For the child with ADHD, sitting still during read-alouds may be a challenge and worthy of much praise. For the social butterfly in your class, the challenge may be to stay focused on independent work rather than chatting with neighbors. On the other hand, you may be encouraging your student with social anxiety to hold a conversation with their peers. It is almost impossible to implement a public behavior chart in a way that promotes equity, meeting each student where their needs lie. If it is necessary to track and report each child's behavioral progress, it is much more kind to utilize a more private and individualized approach, such as a behavior journal or report. This approach can be solution-focused and be used to build relationships and trust.

While classroom management will never be a simple topic to address, and the complexities of developing a relationship with students and building community do not lend themselves easily to step-by-step or one-size-fits all solutions, the effort put into creating a culture of kindness in your classroom is well worth it. By focusing your interactions with students on transformational kindness, balancing high expectations with empathy, and being solution-minded, you will develop trust and have a happier learning environment. These strategies can help make school a joy.

5

Kindness in Teaching

My seventh- and eighth-grade science teacher was Ms. Linda Cook. Before seventh grade, I was indifferent to science, generally preferring English/language arts and reading. Then I met Ms. Cook. She came to class each day with such enthusiasm for her subject that we all couldn't help but be excited about the wonders of the world. Through her class, I learned about not only chemical and physical bonds but also how to take notes in a lecture, think scientifically, and see the true beauty of the natural world. She took us on field trips and accompanied us to the district science fair, letting us into her life. And she was the person who introduced me to the Douglas Adams books, and The Hitchhiker's Guide to the Galaxy *quickly became my favorite book in eighth grade. Because of her influence, I pursued my love of science, attending the Texas Academy of Mathematics and Science in high school and becoming a social science/educational researcher. And I still chat with her on Facebook to this day.*

As we consider kindness in our classroom, perhaps instruction is not an intuitive place to ponder. However, kindness towards content areas is an important part of creating a culture of care and transformational kindness within any community of learning. Additionally, the ways in which we teach and our instructional methods convey kindness (or lack thereof) to our students. Using the lens of transformational kindness to view our instructional choices provides an opportunity for us, as educators, to change our classrooms into inspiring places of joy for learning, much like Ms. Cook's science classroom.

DOI: 10.4324/9781003250739-5

Kindness Towards Our Content Areas

The first step in bringing joy to your teaching is developing (or rediscovering!) transformational kindness toward your content area. Maybe you are a generalist, who has a passion for math lessons, but teaching reading bores you to tears. Maybe you began your career with a passion for Biology, but after 15 years in the classroom, you have forgotten why it is even remotely interesting! Perhaps you are a novice teacher with a deep love for US history, but you have been assigned seven sections of civics to teach. Or maybe you love your content area, but you are bored to tears with the preparation for state accountability tests, the state-mandated curriculum, or the textbook chosen by state officials.

As the graduate program director at my university's teacher preparation department, I get to meet teachers at every level and in every content area. And I have heard more than one of them in each of the above scenarios. Even as an elementary art teacher (one of the most fun jobs ever!), I struggled to find joy in teaching clay sculpture. (That stuff is so messy, dust permeates the room, and there is no saving your hands from the dryness!)

So, my friends, colleagues, readers, I am going to challenge you. This is an exercise that I do with my teacher candidates when they are hitting the hump of the middle of the semester. Think of your absolute least favorite content area or unit—this can come from when you were a student or from your experiences as a teacher. Now, think of three reasons why students should be excited to learn about it. Turn that list into a 30-second "elevator pitch" for your chosen topic. Try this activity in a group, each trying to find more and more traditionally unpopular content areas to "sell" to the others! While it may seem like a silly exercise, it does help to illustrate how every topic has redeeming qualities and can be exciting.

Algebra—what a wonderful opportunity to solve puzzles and use higher-level thinking! English literature—how cool is it that the themes of these novels, plays, and poetry are still relevant today? Plus, reading, this is actually a thing people do for fun!

Biology—the study of how life works, perfect for anyone who is self-absorbed! History—nothing more than an epic drama filled with intrigue and plot twists! You get the idea.

In our undergraduate teacher preparation program, I teach the assessment course. Needless to say, my students are rarely excited to see this one appear on their plans of study. And, while I am on my 20th consecutive semester of teaching this course, it is my goal to approach each class session with enthusiasm and joy. I want my students not just to gain a new perspective about the content and understand the importance and relevance of my content but also to enjoy the experience of exploring the ideas. My favorite student comment left on my evaluations is "Dr. Wilson takes such a horrible course topic and makes it fun and interesting." So, if I can make assessment interesting to undergraduate students, you can find passion for anything you are teaching!

Authenticity to Content

> In fourth grade, we were studying economics and the concepts of supply and demand. To provide an authentic experience around these ideas, our teachers organized an "Entrepreneurship Day" for each of us to start our own business. During the next month, we worked on business plans and created products or services to sell to our classmates. To reward good behavior throughout the month, our teachers gave us "Bronco Bucks" that we could spend on the big day. I remember selling marshmallows on popsicle sticks and dipped in chocolate and sprinkles, but I priced them too high and did not sell very many. (I wasn't all that worried about the lack of success: it meant that I had plenty of candy to eat on the way home!) It was clear that my supply was greater than the demand for the product and thus the value of my product was lower than expected. On the other hand, my best friend had made a limited number of friendship bracelets (man, those take forever to make!). She sold out within minutes, and certainly could have raised her prices, because those fourth graders would have paid almost anything to get their

hands on those! Now, when I think about economics and the market, I still think about marshmallows and friendship bracelets.

As our school systems face increasing pressures to perform on state-mandated achievement tests, the curriculum taught (particularly for our most vulnerable and at-risk students) has become increasingly narrow. The focus on test preparation has done a disservice to both the humans in our classroom and our pedagogy. I recently had a conversation with a middle school principal who mentioned that they no longer include reading novels in their English/language arts curriculum, because they do not meet the standards! Where is the joy of reading if it is not in a great book? It certainly is not reading comprehension passages followed by five multiple choice questions for weeks on end. In fact, that sounds like a recipe for ending any type of love for literature.

Similarly, when we teach history, highlighting only the successes of the United States or Western culture, we lose the interesting details that make the rich story of our past engaging and we also lose important lessons of our past. In his book, *Lies My Teacher Told Me: Everything Your American History Textbooks Got Wrong*, Loewen puts it clearly: "If you truly want students to take an interest in American history, then stop lying to them" (p. 10).

As a system and as teachers, we have to navigate a path that balances the dimensions of state assessments and standards with our own expertise of authentic content. Some teachers are lucky enough to be in a school in which they can shut their classroom door and teach according to their own expertise or, even better, in a school system that encourages and supports innovative pedagogy. If you are in this situation, take advantage of your freedom! Too often, we get into a teaching rut, continuing the same way we always have, relying heavily on textbooks, teaching guides, or ready-made curricula. You have the power to change this—find ways to engage your students in constructing their own knowledge, problem-solving, and authentic learning.

For those of you, like me, in systems that have strong top-down hierarchies or (as most recently in Florida) state regulations about what is taught in your classrooms, I understand your potential frustration. When we are not offered choice, our own professionalism can feel undermined. The negotiations between your integrity towards good pedagogy and the mandated content from state agencies can be treacherous. However, in all cases (even in states that legislate what can and cannot be said in classrooms!), there are ways to incorporate authentic and meaningful content into your lessons and practice. But transformational kindness in schools and classrooms must include kindness towards the content by providing material that is authentic to the discipline. This is transformational kindness towards our content area and has lasting positive effects on our communities.

Authenticity to your content area might include highlighting the voices of people of color in your history or English/language arts classes, including diversity of thought and perspectives to the narratives that are told. It might include reading contemporary young adult novels to increase student engagement in English class, coding in mathematics class, or hands-on experiments in science class. You might use the local biology and ecosystems to connect students with the topics in class or local historical sites for your history class. In any case, authenticity, project-based learning, and inclusive curricula engage students in ways that highlight the excitement and passion that you have for your content area.

When you are able to practice transformational kindness towards your content, your students and the classroom community benefit. This is how we can change the world through our classrooms and help prepare our students for their futures in academic, civic, and career pursuits.

Accountability Test Preparation

> When my oldest daughter was finishing eighth grade, they had the first large-scale writing exam from the state since elementary school. It was the first standardized test of the testing season, and being part of an honors program at their school (James Weldon Johnson College Preparatory Middle School, otherwise known as JWJ),

most of the students were pretty anxious about getting a high score. The night before the test, their teacher, Ms. Mollie Peterson, sent the following group message to the students:

> "I know you will do an incredible job tomorrow morning. I am very proud of the sophistication and detail of your writing. Do your best, but don't stress. It's one moment in a LIFETIME of moments. You are "JWJ"—you'll be great. P.S. Don't forget to plan.:)"

I remember my child coming out of their room to show me the message, and their face lighting up, knowing that it was going to be okay. They did, in fact, do well on the upcoming writing assessment, but more importantly, they learned a valuable truth about kindness and their value versus the importance of the state exam. And Ms. Peterson communicated her care for each of her students, supporting them as people and giving them confidence in the background of instruction that she had instilled in them throughout the year. Every time one of my children goes into a high-stakes test, I try to remind them of Ms. Peterson's words—this is just a moment in a lifetime of moments, and you are part of an amazing group of people and you are loved.

In our current era of education, with the emphasis on accountability as measured by state-mandated testing, the pressures put on schools, teachers, and ultimately students can create environments that fall short of caring and safe spaces. As we, as an educational system, stress the importance of high performance on a single measure of achievement, students can internalize this pressure in unhealthy ways. In the worst cases, this leads to anxiety and increases in mental health crises (e.g., Högberg & Horn, 2022). But it can also lead to less engagement in learning, feelings of isolation, and lack of belonging or indifference (Jones, 2007). Overemphasis on testing and the accountability culture of schools leads to high-stress environments and has detrimental effects on student health (Heissel et al., 2021).

However, we cannot merely ignore the high-stakes assessments, as we are also teaching and nurturing young people in a system in which these tests have important and life-changing consequences attached. Students who do not perform well are held back from advancement to the next grade level, leading to lower graduation rates (Giano et al., 2022), or are placed in remedial coursework that is repetitive and denies them access to other curricular opportunities (e.g., the arts as electives in secondary schools). There are, indeed, academic and social costs associated with poor performance on the state accountability assessments. In many school systems, doing well on the state exams provides access to advanced and college preparatory programs, such as early algebra, Advanced Placement (AP), or honors coursework. These opportunities can lead to more access to higher education and career possibilities (e.g., Gurantz, 2021).

In order to practice transformational kindness, teachers have a responsibility to prepare our students for these assessments and the standards that they assess. But we can approach this in a way that demonstrates care to our students and love for our content. Dr. Popham (2001) makes the distinction between "teaching to the test" or curriculum-teaching and "teaching the test" or item-teaching. I find this a helpful way of framing this issue. In short, teachers can teach the curriculum, preparing students for the content of the tests, without sacrificing their integrity by focusing their efforts on specific items or utilizing only test preparation materials in their courses.

In practice, this means we must find a balance between preparing students, so they have self-efficacy and confidence in approaching high-stakes testing, and providing authentic and engaging instruction that meets the needs of the whole person. Think back to Ms. Peterson: it is really about preparing for testing season through high-quality instruction that aligns with the state standards, incorporating high expectations for student achievement, and giving them the self-confidence to succeed. The approach of comprehensive instruction coupled with a tad of direct instruction on what to expect on test day (i.e., practice with test layout and item types, review of procedures) and test-taking skills (i.e., eliminating obviously wrong distractors, reading questions first, etc.) will boost student's self-efficacy.

Every class is different, so the balance between these activities and how much direct test preparation each group will need changes over the years. The most important thing to keep in mind is that learning content (as opposed to scoring well on an exam) is the ultimate goal of any instruction. Our students are human beings who need confidence, assurance, and safety in order to perform at their best.

Meeting the Needs of Individuals

Differentiated Instruction

Differentiated instruction, or adapting content, product, and/or process of lessons for students' interest, readiness, or ways of learning (Tomlinson, 2001), has become something of a buzzword in educational circles over the last 20 years. However, it seems to be in direct conflict with the emphasis on standardized testing and using the same assessments to measure growth for every student. How can we differentiate for instruction while knowing that our evaluation depends on the same measure for every student, despite their language background, developmental level, or beginning-of-the-year content knowledge and readiness?

However, as we think about the circumstances of the students we teach, the imperative to differentiate becomes even more apparent. Early childhood teachers are experts at this concept, knowing that developmentally the children are at varying stages—some are ready to take their first steps while others in the same classroom are just learning to crawl. As toddlers, some children are fascinated by the alphabet and eager to start on the path to reading (like my youngest, who made a beeline to the magnetic letters every morning at drop-off), while others are busy expanding their large motor skills through climbing, running, and tricycling (like my best friend's youngest, who hasn't met a baby gate that can keep them out of the kitchen). In early-years classrooms, teachers can provide opportunities for all the tiny humans in the learning environment to develop at their current readiness level and interests. However, if we jump forward a couple of years, our system expects all of the students to be at the same development level and respond to the same instructional strategies. Are all 5-year-olds ready to read in September? Are all 18-year-olds ready to be on their own and in college in May?

Given the many pressures they face, a classroom teacher cannot be expected to provide high-quality individualized learning to every student. (However, if you have figured out how to complete this heroic task, please drop me a line—I am sure we could bottle this up and make a ton of money!) In all seriousness, it is a struggle to balance the curriculum goals set forward in grade-level standards and the diverse needs in a typical classroom. The principles of differentiation offer opportunities for teachers to bring kindness, honoring the unique learning needs of individuals while being kind to the limitations of being a human being yourself.

Differentiated instruction involves flexible grouping rather than designing lessons for each individual learner. For example, I might be doing a unit on life during the American colonial era, and I could group students by interest for their projects (e.g., sports, clothing/fashion, food, hobbies/crafts, and schools). On the other hand, I might group students by ways of learning and expressing their understanding, by having one group work on making a video, another on a written newspaper, and perhaps another on painting a mural about the way of life during the colonial era. Finally, I could group students by their reading level, giving each group highly engaging primary source documents that align with their readiness level in reading. For the next unit on the American Revolutionary War, I could differentiate in different ways, to ensure that students have the opportunity to work in a variety of groups with different peer groups. In this way, I am providing for diverse learning needs but in a manageable way. I do not have 30 individual lessons to plan, only shifts for three to four groups.

Differentiated instruction based upon achievement, ability, or readiness level often makes educators uncomfortable because of the connotations with strict tracking of students or concerns of equality for all learners. To address tracking, educators must use flexible grouping. This means that grouping by achievement level and background knowledge is only one of several ways that you group for instruction. It is also important to pre-assess often, rearranging groups based upon the specific skills and content knowledge for specific lessons and units. A student who struggles with computational skills in elementary math may excel in geometry units because of their spatial reasoning skills. Children who do not have background knowledge about simple machines may have a wealth of knowledge about plants and life cycles. Thus, teachers and school systems can avoid tracking or pigeon-holing students when ability grouping by using continual assessments and creating multiple opportunities to move between groups and levels.

There is also a misconception that fairness in schools involves providing the same resources, instruction, and evaluation to all students. However, true equity (versus equality) occurs when we provide differentiated resources based upon the needs of each student (or groups of students). For example, if all students are working on a problem-solving task, some students will need additional scaffolding to frame the problem and develop a solution, while other students will need opportunities to expand their thinking and additional challenges to the problem. By providing both scaffolding and extensions within the same open-ended project, teachers can help ensure equity—that every student's needs will be met during the instructional period.

Taken a step further, this could mean that one group of students in a classroom is working on an advanced project while another group is focusing on the fundamental skills for the unit. Equity in this scenario is to ensure that both groups are assigned engaging and meaningful work, at differentiated levels. In this way, the individual is honored by experiencing success in their learning, being challenged at appropriate levels, and can learn and grow in the curriculum. If all students in the class had the same assignment, some would be overwhelmed and unable to access the content while others would be unchallenged and not grow through the lessons they had already mastered. Imagine if the teachers in the infant room insisted that every baby work on learning how to crawl—even the ones who were ready to walk! Or, conversely, if the baby who just learned how to roll over was forced to try to take their first steps. Of course, that would be a disaster.

Transformational kindness is adapting curricula both up and down to ensure that all people in the learning environment have the opportunity to learn something new every day.

When you design tiered lessons or differentiated units, it is vital that all learners have access to engaging learning opportunities. Each group should feel valued, honored, and seen in the learning community. For example, if the students who need more scaffolding are resigned to skill-based worksheets while the more advanced learners are building and creating models (or, vice versa, the students who need more help get manipulatives while the advanced students "get" to write a paper), there is not equity and one group of students will not feel valued. Instead, teachers could work to create tiered learning experiences that respect and engage all learners.

Of course, there have been many excellent books and professional learning courses written about differentiation, and it would be impossible to cover all aspects and nuances of this strategy in a few pages of this book. So, I encourage you to explore the resources listed at the back of this book.

Universal Design for Learning

A similar and complementary approach to differentiated instruction is Universal Design for Learning (UDL). UDL is a framework and lens for instruction that encourages teachers to design learning environments that are accessible for all learners. In this approach, the educator provides supports for every person in the community. These can be simple, like ensuring closed captioning for videos—to support deaf and hard-of-hearing students but also students with auditory processing disorders. For all students, the captioning can help with comprehension and reading skills. Instruction utilizing multiple modalities (e.g., visual, auditory, and hands-on) has similar effects. By adopting UDL, the needs of students, including students with exceptionalities, can be met without having to publicly announce any student's individual differences.

Open-ended projects that allow opportunities for learners to respond at their level of understanding are further examples of UDL. In this case, all learners may be creating a poster, writing an essay, or delivering a speech, but they can engage at their level. English language learners may rely more on visual aides to explain their learning, advanced students have the opportunity to explore a topic in more depth, and students with specific learning disabilities can fulfill the assignment to their abilities. All students are respected and have access to the assignment, and the teacher can facilitate a caring and safe learning environment. Again, using UDL in the classroom could be a book in and of itself, so please find more resources in the back of this book.

Specific Interventions

As an educator in today's world, you encounter students from diverse linguistic, cultural, educational, and cognitive backgrounds. These experiences are often quite different from our own. Engaging in professional learning for English language learners, exceptional or special education, LGBTQ safe spaces, gifted learners, and culturally relevant teaching can also help us to be better equipped to address the needs and celebrate the differences in our classrooms. While I do not have the space to include strategies for Multi-Tiered Levels of Support (MTSS), Response to Intervention (RTI), diversity, language development, and safe spaces in this text, I have assembled resources on these topics at the end of the book.

Specifically, as educators, we show transformational kindness when we take time to develop our own understandings about special populations and apply this knowledge to our practice in schools and classrooms. By listening to members of diverse communities, being vulnerable to learn more, and not being content with our current levels of understanding, we can demonstrate in real ways that our learning spaces are safe and welcome to all.

As we consider our pedagogy and instructional practices as educators, we are reminded of the tremendous responsibility with which we are entrusted. Thinking of our curricular and instructional decisions through the lens of transformational kindness results in changes to how we approach teaching. This provides opportunities for us to consider how these decisions affect our students and how we can design experiences to ensure that the human beings in our classrooms feel safe, included, and valued as members of our community.

Assessment

> My freshman year of college, I took a religion class at my small liberal arts college. Dr. Steve Stell held high expectations for the course, wanting each of us to deeply understand the concepts of faith, spirituality, and the history of Christianity. But, like all my professors at Austin College, he valued the relationships that were built between faculty and students. I remember the urban legend of him taking a class "field trip" to a certain senior's dorm room when he did not show up for class one morning, thus ensuring that the student would be in class and not miss instruction, much to the delight of the rest of the class. But what struck me the most was his approach to midterms and finals. Rather than call them "exams," Dr. Stell titled each of them "celebrations of learning"—assuring us that these were opportunities for us to show off what we had learned and to celebrate our accomplishments. I have since adopted this practice in my courses, changing the mindset of the exam from punitive and demanding to appreciative and celebratory.

As we reflect on classroom assessments, transformational kindness is probably not the first thing that comes to mind. However, assessment in the learning environment presents an excellent opportunity for educators to demonstrate their care of and respect to their students.

Classroom Tests and Quizzes

Just like Dr. Stell, we can change our framework for understanding classroom assessments from one of accountability to one of celebration. Instead of using tests to "catch" students in what they do not know or remember, we can use tests to take joy in what they have accomplished. We can design items that are difficult, perhaps, but not tricky—designed to evaluate their knowledge and skills but not to trip them up on small mistakes.

I teach guidelines for test item development to my graduate and undergraduate teacher candidates. Here are some of the top examples:

1. **Avoid using words like "not" or "except" in test items**. These words are easy to miss, especially for English language learners or students with reading disabilities, and we don't usually need to assess when something isn't a part of a category, group, and so on.
2. **Avoid trivia**. Sometimes our test items include information that is just not all that important to the overall unit or lesson. Do students really need to know the exact date of a battle, or is it more important for them to know which battle came first?
3. **True/false items—Just say no**. These items tend to be difficult to understand, relying on very nuanced understandings of the English language, putting English language learners at a disadvantage. Also, gifted and advanced learners tend to overthink them and also get them wrong!
4. **Keep the questions long and the choices short**. When writing selected choice items (multiple choice, matching, etc.), put as much information in the item stem or question as possible, leaving the choices short and concise. This will lessen the amount that a student must read to understand the question. Ideally, a student should be able to read the question and answer it without reading the answer choices. When testing vocabulary, put the definitions in the questions and leave the words as the answer choices, or in matching, put the definitions in the left-hand column.

5. **Put the answer choices in a logical order**. Alphabetize names, put numbers and dates in order, and so on. This makes it easier for students to find the answer they know is correct.

I know some of these sound like common sense, but, seriously, when I look at the exams that some of my colleagues across the university write, I am amazed at the lack of attention to detail.

If you have ever been on the receiving end of a "pop quiz," you probably already understand the stress and anxiety that it can produce. Particularly when educators use these types of assessments to "catch" students who have not been studying, paying attention in class, or doing the readings, these unannounced quizzes can harm the community of the classroom and break down the trust that students have in their teacher. If you want to keep students accountable for their reading, homework, or classwork, why not have regularly scheduled quizzes, so that students can adequately prepare for them? This demonstrates much more kindness towards each student.

Similarly, I have overheard more than one teacher use quizzes, tests, and exams as threats or punishments for students. "If you keep talking, we will have a quiz next class period" or "You better pay attention, or this is going to be on your exam." Sigh. It is no wonder that so many of our children develop test anxiety—we are teaching them to fear them!

Transformational kindness means that educators will celebrate with students the learning that has occurred during a unit and use the exams as ways for students to show off what they have accomplished. I like to add a question at the end of each exam that simply says, "What did you learn in this unit that I didn't ask on this exam?" This gives students an opportunity to share their learning and celebrate with me.

Formative Assessments

I start every semester of my assessment course by telling my teacher candidates that in a classroom we are almost always assessing our students. Sometimes that is formal assessment, by giving a test or a quiz. Sometimes it is through instruction, like when we are doing a project. But most of the time, it is informally. When I am giving a lecture, I am assessing my students—are they paying attention? Do I need to give them a break to stretch their legs? Do they look confused, do I need to clarify a point? When I lead a discussion, I am assessing their conversations. Are they on topic? Do they have misunderstandings? What should I clarify or explain? By framing assessment as something that we, as educators, constantly engage in, I help them to see how it also informs every part of our instruction.

When I mention formative assessment, most educators think about pre-tests and the diagnostic testing that they use to put students in groups or differentiate instruction. But, if we go back to the definition that you may or may not remember from your education coursework, it really means any type of assessment that *informs* our instructional practice. In this way, most of what we do in a classroom can be considered formative assessment.

In fact, I would argue that to conduct an assessment in a classroom but not use it for instructional decisions is not ethical. Why put students through a test, taking away from their instructional time, if we are not going to use that information to help them in their learning? (This is a question I would like to pose to many of the decision makers about the state-funded accountability testing as well.)

What does this look like in practice? It means that we are doing continual assessments, giving students check-ins, exit tickets, quizzes, or journal entries to assess their understandings. Then we are adjusting our instruction, our groupings, and our pacing accordingly.

We can include both formal and informal assessments in this planning. It might be a on-the-spot adjustment to a lesson or small group when it is clear the students are not grasping a concept. Or it could be re-teaching a lesson or unit after poor scores on an exam or quiz. In either case, transformational kindness means utilizing assessment data to benefit the children in our classrooms and schools.

Use of Assessment Data

Some districts and school systems have adopted the term "data-driven decision-making" as if something as impersonal and as easily manipulated as data should or could make all our decisions in schools and classrooms. I much prefer the term "data-informed decision-making" which implies that human beings are making decisions using data but also other sources of information, like best practices, care and kindness, and cultural awareness.

Children are not computers in which we can dump information, nor are they numbers in a spreadsheet that can be manipulated. Children are living, breathing human beings, and it takes information about their whole being to teach them. Sure, test scores and assessment data can give us information to plan our lessons, but we must not give up all of our human abilities to demonstrate transformational kindness and consider the whole child.

For example, a student who made high marks throughout the year, scored well on the mid-year assessments, and demonstrated understanding of the course material in class, but experienced a trauma the week before the state end-of-year exam, should be treated with compassion and care. Depending on the circumstances and how they cope over the summer, the remedial courses that their scores on the exam would normally indicate are most likely not an appropriate placement for the next school year. Data-driven decision-making would put them in a remedial class, focusing on basic skills. Data-informed decision-making would allow re-testing or placement in a standard or advanced course based upon additional sources of information and in consultation with the school counselor or psychologist.

Performance Assessments

> If I asked you to remember a specific test or exam that you took in school, you probably would struggle. Maybe you remember taking the SATs or a state-mandated exam, but likely the specifics elude you. Now, if I asked you to remember a project that you completed in school, you can probably recall quite a bit of detail about what

> you learned, even going back to elementary school. For example, in fifth grade, we were studying the Renaissance, and I did a project on the Black Death. My display was a tri-fold board with the silhouette of an Italian city, black rats were strategically placed along the edges of building and coming out of doorways, and a cart of lifeless bodies was rolling through the abandoned streets. A diagram of a large flea adorned the top of the display, with critical facts about the transmission of bubonic plague, and I can still tell you that over a third of the European population died as a result of the disease.

We, as educators, have the unique opportunity to give our students lasting memories and lifelong learning through projects. Performance assessments (sometimes called alternative assessments) beautifully combine instruction and assessment, and they are some of my favorite instructional tools. Practicing transformational kindness means providing students with engaging assessments that instruct as well as evaluate. They also allow you to guide students throughout the journey, providing support and extensions as necessary to tailor the experiences to individual and group needs.

Project-based learning, or an approach that eschews traditional assessments entirely in favor of performance-based assessments, has gained popularity among charter and specialized schools, in reaction to the accountability culture that pervades the majority of our school system. This approach, though extreme, provides students with the chance to explore topics in-depth and develop problem-solving skills. Used in combination with techniques such as the Socratic Seminar, 5-E Inquiry Approach, and Paideia Seminars, this approach can engage students in higher-order thinking, critical reasoning, and creative thinking. See the Resources section to find more information on these topics.

Authentic assessments are useful within the performance assessment category, as they relate the project to the real-life work of the discipline. This can increase engagement and relevancy for students. It also can help students to think creatively to solve problems in their local context. This can be exploring fractions and percentages by calculating the compound interest for a car loan and deciding whether or not it is economically sound to buy that Ford Mustang convertible. Or it can be exploring the local ecosystem and designing a project to lower the human impact on the environment.

While we often associate authentic assessments with secondary school students getting ready to enter the adult world, I have seen early childhood teachers utilizing this strategy with great success. The pre-kindergarten class at my university lab school studied the migration patterns and habitats of butterflies. Then they worked together to plan and build a butterfly garden in their playscape outside. Together this class of 4-year-olds had an authentic experience of researching, planning, and executing a garden. And through this transformational experience, the teachers and the school demonstrated kindness, not only to the students but to the entire school community who got to enjoy the garden.

Through our assessments, our instructional strategies, and our classroom management, we show our care and compassion for students. As educators, we have the chance to use transformational kindness in our classrooms and schools every day to make a positive change in the world. Through our actions, we model the kindness that our students will learn from, feel included by, and (hopefully) live out in their daily lives as well.

6

Kindness Towards Your Community

Each year, the elementary school hosts a fall carnival, complete with bouncy houses, trick-or-treating in the classrooms, party games, inflatable slides, and costumed parent volunteers. It is the highlight of the school year and a huge fundraiser for the school. But the best part about the annual event is the community involvement. I love seeing the middle school and high school alumni from the neighborhood return to the school to participate—either to volunteer or just to say hi to their teachers and hang out with their friends. I love seeing young families, with children not yet old enough to attend kindergarten, push their strollers down the sidewalk on the way to the school and grandparents with their charges in hand making their way to the playground.

Whether we, as educators, work as school administrators, teachers, or support staff, we have a responsibility to our greater community, including the families and neighborhoods. While we prioritize our relationship-building with students and co-workers, the larger community is also vital to a well-functioning and kind school. When a school demonstrates care to the community, everyone is encouraged to feel safe, loved, and valuable—just like at the community carnival in my neighborhood.

Schools are foundational to a community, whether it is the neighborhood elementary school playground, the high school football game, or the junior high marching band during the annual city parade. Schools can be a stabilizing force for generations, a source of employment, and a point of pride for struggling and thriving communities alike. Schools provide a hub for

DOI: 10.4324/9781003250739-6

community engagement, a common space, and a resource for neighborhoods. When educators become part of the community, it benefits everyone.

Parents and Families

As a teacher of young human beings, we have the enormous responsibility of caring for a member of someone else's family. We are entrusted to educate, protect, and nurture a child who is loved unconditionally by someone else. For the child's family, your student is the center of their world, the most important member of your classroom. And both you and the family have the common goal of nurturing the child for the school year. But parent and family conflict with educators is universal—and many educators feel unprepared for family communication and involvement.

The first impression that you make on a family can be the most important interaction you have with them. It is vital to communicate a collaborative outlook in which you value families and partnerships in your learning community. When I was a teacher, I made a goal to speak to each and every parent by the first month of school to share a good report about their student. By communicating something that I appreciate about their child, I could start the relationship off on a positive note—demonstrating my care for the student and family. Trust me, finding a good moment to share for some of members of my classroom community could be challenging (especially for a novice teacher!). But focusing on those positive traits also helped me to change my mindset about my classroom. I saw an internal shift in my own attitude as well as increased parental engagement and support. Later in the year, if I needed to address an issue with the family regarding a student, I had already established a positive relationship.

Family Conferences and Communication

I hear from many educators that they dread parent/teacher or family conferences. Whether it is a general apprehension about talking with adults (versus the children they interact with on a daily basis), conflict avoidance, or prioritizing other aspects of their work over family communication, family conferences never seem to be on the top of any educator's list.

Additionally, teacher preparation programs do not necessarily include much support for teacher candidates to practice these interactions before becoming the instructor of record in a school classroom. But families and teachers form the two most important adult communities in a child's life and working together they can transform the trajectory for a child and create spaces in which every child can be nurtured and grow to their greatest potential.

Approaching family conferences and communications with a lens of transformational kindness means that you are seeing every person in the dynamic (family members, students, and teachers) as valuable people with both strengths and areas for improvement. All parents and families (except perhaps in extreme cases of abuse or neglect) want the best for their children, and even when we, as educators, do not personally agree with their choices, we can appreciate our common ground. Although we might go about bringing out the best futures for the child in different ways and from different perspectives, all parties are working for the best outcomes for the child.

Families know more about the student than we could ever learn in the short amount of time that we get to spend with the child, and their insights are valuable in creating learning spaces that are nurturing to the student. Transformational kindness consists of listening carefully to families and including them in the classroom community.

Conflicts with Family

When called to a conference, many families respond with immediate defensiveness. It is a natural instinct for a caretaker to protect their child, and when they feel threatened, they may react negatively towards the teacher. This is particularly true if the family members themselves had negative experiences in schools or if their interactions with their children's schools have been hostile in the past. For an educator and member of the school community, who also wants what is best for the child, approaching family conferences and communications with empathy and compassion is of utmost importance. I try to begin each meeting or communication emphasizing the common ground and understandings that we share. By assuring families that you are there for the child and demonstrating that care, you can work to build trust for all the adults in each student's life.

Unfortunately, for many families, prior experiences may have broken down their trust in the school system, and as members of that (sometimes) broken system, we will have to work extra hard to build that trust.

Strategies for Family Conferences

For educators who are nervous about family conferences, having specific strategies for conferences can provide structure and help alleviate some of the stress. These strategies are ways in which educators can approach meetings with families to help these conferences be more productive and friendly and to demonstrate transformational kindness.

Prior to the meeting, it is important to be upfront and clear about its purpose. If you are the one requesting the meeting, be sure to communicate whether your concerns are behavioral or academic, you are eliciting the help of the family to develop solutions, or you want to communicate about progress towards goals. When families know what to expect in the conference, they will feel less anxious and defensive and they can be prepared. Additionally, they will have time to process any immediate negative reactions to the situation. No one likes a surprise attack, so be sure to start with clear communication to build trust with families, and practice transformational kindness.

If the family is requesting the meeting, attempt to schedule it as soon as possible and gently ask for as much information about the purpose of the meeting as possible. The more you know what to expect, the more prepared you can be and you will also have time to process any initial emotions and reactions. Depending on the family, you may not get all of the information you would like prior to the meeting, but the most important thing to remember is to stay upbeat in communications. Ensure that your communications nurture communities that are welcoming to families.

During the conference, it is likely that you will need to communicate negative aspects of the child's performance, issues with behavior, or areas of weakness. Remembering that you are discussing this family's pride and joy, someone that they love deeply and unconditionally, this must be done in a way that continues to emphasize the common goals of the best interest of the student. Even disciplinary meetings can (and should) be done in the best interest of the student, asking how we can work together to teach the child better ways to behave and change the trajectory of their actions.

"Sandwich compliments" are a starting point for a novice teacher to address issues with families. Using this technique, you start with a positive statement, give feedback about a problem, and then end with another compliment. Thus, you are making a "sandwich" of feedback. This can help families understand that you also want to see the good things about the child and care about them and their success.

Additional Support

As a classroom teacher, you may encounter families that are particularly hostile or argumentative. In these cases, it can be helpful to have additional support for meetings. If there is a team of teachers who work with the student, you could consider a group approach. School administrators, counselors, psychologists, and social workers can also provide more support and perspective. If there is a team of educators to advocate for the child, the family's behavior can be monitored to keep everyone safe. This helps to protect you from potential verbal abuse and from being accused of untrue behaviors or statements. Finally, the saying, "two heads are better than one" rings true—by bringing together a solution-oriented team, a solution can appear that would not have come together with only one member of the team. Teachers with more experience, professionals trained in psychology and behavior, and administrators with experience in leadership can often develop solutions and defuse tense situations.

Diversity in the Community

For many of us in the teaching profession, the lived experiences of our students and the communities in which they exist are very different from our own. This means that the expectations of behavior, the role of schools and teachers, and communication styles can vary greatly. For example, for some families, the teacher is the ultimate authority and expert; thus, they should not interfere or be involved in school activities. Their lack of school engagement might be out of reverence and respect. For other communities, there might be differences in body language, tone of voice, personal space, or use of formal language. This can cause us, as outsiders to the community or visitors to a neighborhood, to place our own judgments and assumptions on the communication from families. When we enter a new community, it can take a while to learn the nuances of communication and the cultural norms.

As an education professional, working within the lens of transformational kindness, we are best serving our students when we approach every interaction by assuming the best intentions of all parties. For example, the parent who may appear underdressed for school pick-up feels comfortable enough in your school community to dress casually. The parent who raises his voice on a phone call home has passion and care to defend their child. The family that does not attend Open House may be embarrassed by their lack of education or busy making ends meet or maybe they did not receive the communications sent home. The caregivers who do not sign notes sent home or fill out school forms may be coping with their own trauma, mental illness, or life stressors. By adopting an unconditional human regard to the families in our schools, we practice compassion and empathy that ultimately benefits everyone.

Because public schools are open for all children (maybe one of the greatest institutions in our world), we have the radical charge to educate all students and support families from all backgrounds. This means that sometimes our personal values may not align with the families of our students. In our increasingly politically divided society, this can create conflict over how to best educate our students. As educators, we have to tread these lines carefully, honoring and respecting the family's personal views while providing high-quality education. For the most part, we can approach conflicts in values with kindness and respect, agreeing to disagree on topics.

For example, for a student who has a religious belief that prevents them from participating in holiday celebrations, teachers can offer alternative arrangements, working with the family to honor and respect their beliefs, even when they aren't shared by the educator. Similarly, students who are observing religious fasting (as Muslim families do during Ramadan) can be provided with an alternate setting for lunch and snack times. Families and students may object to reciting the Pledge of Allegiance, school dress codes, or school events (such as dances, prom, or extracurricular and co-curricular clubs) for religious, political, or cultural beliefs. Even when school professionals do not share these beliefs, they can work with families and students to accommodate their own child's participation in these activities. Students can stay respectfully seated during the Pledge of Allegiance, wear head coverings during class, or not join the clubs that conflict with their beliefs. As members of a public school system, we have the distinct honor and enormous responsibility to respect and value each and every student and their family that are members of our community.

However, some situations can become more complicated. When a family disagrees with the content of a novel read in class, reasonable modifications can be made for the student to read an alternate selection. But when a family objects to a required standard or learning objective (e.g., human reproduction, evolution, or historical perspectives), the discussion can be tricky. Of course, always rely on the school, district, or state policies to guide decisions. Additional support from school or district leadership can also be helpful to navigate these situations. The most important principle to remember is that your responsibility is to the student, supporting their family, culture, and values to promote safe and healthy learning environments.

Everyone partnering together to nurture and educate the student through adulthood is trying their best to make decisions in the best interest of the student, even when we disagree with these choices. Approaching each of these interactions with transformational kindness, we can seek solutions with the involvement of families.

Sensitive Issues

However, parents' and families' views on education occasionally impede the freedoms and choices for other families and students. For example, while a family may feel that a book discussing sensitive topics (e.g., sexual assault, race discrimination, or gay relationships) is inappropriate for their high school-age student, these topics might be vital for other students to feel heard, accepted, or valued within the community. Educators must take care to honor the wishes of the parent without harming the development of other students. In this example, it would be ideal to work with one set of parents to ensure they feel comfortable with the selection of books their child brought home, but it would be unkind to remove the books for all student access. In my middle school library, back in the 1990s, books with sensitive topics were marked with a blue dot, and parents could opt out of allowing their children to have access to those books, without impeding on the rights and freedoms of other families.

Similarly, offering families options to discuss puberty, sexual development, and birth control or sexually transmitted disease prevention according to their own values and perspectives should not interfere with the school system's responsibility to provide age-appropriate, scientifically based, and practical information to students. It has been shown when children have a vocabulary for body parts and direct instruction about sexual abuse (at developmentally appropriate levels) they are at a lower risk for abuse (Finkelhor, 2007). Therefore, an approach for schools to be silent on these issues, or to acquiesce to individual family interests prohibiting universal discussions of such topics, is inherently dangerous to the general population of students. Instead, it is the kindest approach to continue to provide scientifically based sex education to students while working with individual families to provide alternate experiences when this information conflicts with their values. To deny all children access to this education because of the voice of some families puts our students at risk for teen pregnancy, life-threatening diseases, and sexual abuse (Rabbitte & Enriquez, 2009).

Another sensitive topic for parents, families, and schools is race in our society. While there are families in our communities that object to the historical narrative that includes minority voice (e.g., the atrocities done to Native Americans, the violent struggles for Civil Rights, or the oppression of people of color), these same narratives provide context and explanations for the current state of our society. Redlining in the 1930s and continuing through the 1970s (a policy that explicitly prohibited families of color from purchasing homes in more affluent neighborhoods) explains why a simple "pull yourself up by the bootstraps" approach doesn't fully account for the differences in economic prosperity in the United States. The voices of people of color, and those disenfranchised by our history, give voice to our students and families that face oppression in our current society. By ignoring the realities of our collective histories, we invalidate the historical circumstances that have created inequity today.

Teaching our history, even in our difficult history, helps all students contextualize the current events and be better in the future. When we celebrate Christopher Columbus without recognizing the mass genocide of Native peoples that followed, discuss the patriotic effort during World War II without mentioning the Japanese internment camps, or teach the founding fathers without mentioning slavery, we trivialize the lives of the people who suffered the atrocities of our past and allow the real hurt that caused to generations of Americans to fester. Transformational kindness means recognizing the truths of our history and helping our students put these truths into context.

As teachers, we may be tempted, particularly in the face of community or political pressures, to explain away or ignore the negative aspects of our history. It is all too easy to focus on traditional heroes of our culture—the White male forefathers who dominate the narratives of our textbooks. However, we have a responsibility to the diverse populations that we serve, and the wider society, to portray narratives different from our own and those that give a more complete picture of our society. For more sources on these topics, see the Resources section.

Another group that is left out of many school curricula is the lesbian, gay, bisexual, transgender, and queer (LGBTQ) community. However, we live in a world that includes diverse families, including those with same-gender parents, non-binary and gender-diverse individuals, and non-traditional families. Despite any feelings or beliefs that you, as an individual, may have about these family dynamics, your responsibility is to ensure that every student and every family feels accepted and valued in your learning community.

If you include books that represent various family structures (single-parent, blended, same-sex, extended families, foster families), then all children will know they are welcome and included in your learning space. Similarly, by including books in secondary classroom and school libraries that feature protagonists of diverse gender expressions and sexual orientations, educators communicate the value of LGBTQ individuals in their schools. LGBTQ youth have some of the highest rates of suicide, mental health issues, and homelessness (Klein et al., 2022). You, as an educator, have the power to create a safe place in your classroom for all gender expressions (transgender, non-binary, gender fluid, cisgender, etc.) and sexual orientations (straight, gay, bisexual, asexual, etc.). When students know they have at least one trusted adult in their lives, their risk for self-harm and suicide greatly decreases (Taliaferro & Muehlenkamp, 2017). You can be that person.

When you have a student who has disclosed their sexual or gender identity to you, it is important that you respect their privacy. Before sharing that information with anyone (including the child's family), be sure that you have their permission (GLSEN, 2019), to the extent that this is permissible by your school and district policies. Remember that not all families are accepting and that disclosing this information may put the child at a greater risk for physical and emotional abuse or homelessness. If you feel uncomfortable or feel like you need additional support to help the student, ask whether you can accompany them to share their concerns with a trusted member of the school crisis team, school counselor, or support staff. *Of course, if the child has disclosed that they intend to harm themselves or others, you have the ethical duty to respond by informing your school's crisis team and getting them the help that they need to stay safe.*

Being accepted for their identity is a crucial factor for all students' mental health. Having a school-wide Gay-Straight Alliance (GSA) or other affirming club can provide the support for youth to be healthy and develop in a safe environment. For more information on this topic, see the Resources section.

True transformational kindness is accepting families and children from all communities (even those that are quite different from our own) and showing them radical love and respect. You, as an educator, can feel empowered to try to accommodate learning experiences for each family's values as long as those accommodations do not interfere with another family's or student's freedoms.

Advocacy

Finally, as an educator, we have a responsibility for advocacy for our communities. This could be for individual students or families within a school, for neighborhoods within a school system, or for schools and education at the legislative level. As professionals who have the privilege of advanced education about schools, learning, and children, we have a responsibility as citizens in society to advocate for our profession, students, and schools. Transformational kindness indicates that we need to share our knowledge, skills, and expertise to help others.

Individuals

In our roles working with students and families, we have to advocate for what is best for individuals. This may be during an Individual Education Plan (IEP) meeting to determine the course of services for a student with exceptionalities. You, as the educator, may need to speak up to highlight the student's strengths, argue for more services and support for the student, or represent the student interests.

Families that struggle financially may need an advocate to connect them to school and community resources for nutrition, uniforms or school clothing, supplies, or funds for field trips and other co-curricular and extra-curricular activities.

Families that speak languages other than English may need an advocate who can help them gain access to information from the school.

Students who show advanced skills or learning may need an advocate to help families and schools find appropriate experiences and coursework for them.

Your primary role as a teacher or educator puts you in an ideal position to advocate for the students in your classroom and school. Your voice is important to inspire change for the individuals in your sphere of influence.

Communities

As a teacher, you may find yourself in a position to advocate for a community of students or families. In my local elementary school, a community of refugee families became part of our school. Though largely unfamiliar with the specific cultural norms and the language of the new members of the school community, the teachers worked to advocate for the families—coordinating with community organizations to provide social services and the school community to provide donations to meet the physical needs of the refugee families.

At other times, teachers can advocate for the needs of a community at school board meetings. This could be during budget allocations for more resources at a school (staff, physical facilities, or materials and equipment), programs for a group of students (e.g., English language learners, exceptional education, gifted learners, or students from backgrounds of poverty), or areas of the curriculum (e.g., the arts, physical education, or vocational programs).

Local advocacy might also include reaching out to community organizations and businesses for the school. Local businesses might be able to provide mentors, speakers, or volunteers for schools. Local organizations can partner with schools to raise the profile of the school or provide additional services. For example, as an art teacher, I partnered with our local grocery stores to display student artwork in the community. We also had display areas in the neighborhood library and at city hall.

Local school board elections can make a significant difference in the life and functioning of schools and teachers. It is important for us, as education professionals, to make informed decisions at the ballot box and to share our insights about policy and elections with the community. Transformational kindness is using your own expertise to inform others about issues in your community schools. Be sure that when you engage in this work that you follow the policies of your district and state carefully. Many restrict the use of school resources (e.g., computers and email accounts) to campaign in any elections.

State and National Advocacy

While we can make change by advocating for individual students and families at the local level, the state and national policies have significant influence on the daily life of local schools. Think about the impact of the 2001 No Child Left Behind Act on the school systems, implementing yearly accountability assessments at every grade level, 3rd to 10th, in reading and math. On average, 55% of funding for local schools comes from state and federal sources (Leachman & Figueroa, 2019). When those funds are cut, students, teachers, and families are harmed. For a teacher adopting a framework of transformational kindness, advocating for adequately funded schools becomes imperative. Without a living wage, teachers cannot teach children; without updated technology and facilities, children are at a disadvantage compared with their peers; without adequate supplies, children don't have access to the types of experiences that will prepare them for the future. Our local middle school recently ran out of funds for toilet paper and soap in the bathrooms, speaking to the incredible and overwhelming budget crises of our schools.

Recent state legislative sessions increasing the standardized and high-stakes assessment accountability put additional stressors on school systems. Policies restricting curriculum and limiting the academic freedom of teachers devalue the education and profession and limit access to learning for students. These policies can have negative impacts on schools and children. When policy makes decisions about schools without input from the educator community, the students and schools are harmed. As educators, we must be part of this discourse.

As an individual, you can use the resources in the back of this book to research the education platforms of candidates for state and national elections. You can write letters and set meetings with legislators at state and national levels. When important bills are brought to the state legislature, you can advocate and speak directly to the committee and the legislative body as a whole. I have advocated with my children at legislative sessions on behalf of students who receive financial aid for higher education, LGBTQ students, and gifted services.

However, these actions can be intimidating to take on as an individual. Joining an organization, such as those listed in the Resources section, can help you focus your advocacy efforts and support you. By becoming part of a group, you can amplify your voice and you can support advocacy efforts through the use of trained lobbyists. Specific organizations, such as the National Association for Gifted Children, the Council for Exceptional Children, or the National Art Education Association, provide advocacy for their interests. Additionally, teachers' unions, such as the National Education Association (NEA) and the American Federation of Teachers (AFT), have resources at both national and state levels to help educators be more involved in influencing education policy. Most of these organizations are non-partisan, but you can also find resources that align with your political views. It is important that we cross political lines and ideologies to do what we can collectively to improve the school systems for all students.

While advocacy at individual, local, state, or national levels may not be the first thing that comes to mind when considering transformational kindness for educators, the collective influence of educators to make a positive change in our schools cannot be ignored. We are kind to our communities when we advocate for our students and schools.

As educators, we are members of our community—at our schools, our neighborhoods, and the larger society. Kindness to our communities means honoring and respecting the values and perspectives of students, families, and community members—even when they do not align with our own. It also means that we use our voice and expertise to advocate on their behalf.

We can all work together, through transformational kindness, to make our learning communities, schools, and classrooms places where the entire community, people and families from all backgrounds, can feel welcomed, safe, and included.

7

Kindness Towards Self

For the last chapter of this book, it seemed appropriate that I would end as I began, with references to some of my favorite musicals. Musicals tell stories of personal redemption, teach us how to love ourselves, and give us hope for our futures. In *Rent* (Jonathan Larson), we are asked to "measure our life in love" and practice intentional gratitude for those in life who bring us joy. In *Legally Blonde* (Nell Benjamin), Elle Woods reminds us that "being true to yourself never goes out of style" and that achieving our dreams and goals does not mean that we have to sacrifice our morals and our kindness. And at the end of *Mean Girls* (Nell Benjamin), Janice reminds us that "sometimes what's meant to break us, makes us brave," encouraging us to persevere when times are hard, knowing that we can face the obstacles in front of us.

Although this chapter is the last and shortest in the book, it does not mean that kindness towards self should be last or least in your priorities. As RuPaul says, "If you can't love yourself, how can you love anybody else?" When we practice kindness towards ourselves, we practice transformational kindness to our communities.

Education is a service profession, and most (if not all) of us joined the field because we wanted to help others, to show kindness, and to make a positive difference in the lives of our

DOI: 10.4324/9781003250739-7

students. However, with this generous and caring spirit, we can forget that we must prioritize self-care, and true kindness to ourselves, or we risk burn-out, unhealthy boundaries, and (at the least) not being our best selves. In order for us to be able to give to others, our own needs must be met.

The Basics

> Late in 2020, I'll be honest, I was struggling. Depression had hit me hard, and as I watched many of the relationships around me deteriorate, I found myself having difficulty getting out of bed and taking care of the basic tasks of life. And, suddenly, my best friend moved into action. Even though Jill was several states away and taking care of three children of her own, she took the time each day to text me, checking in, and reminding me to take care of myself. Her simple acts of kindness reminded me each day to take time to get out of the house, take deep breaths, and, if nothing else, take a shower and eat a meal. Jill was my lifeline in a difficult time and (along with a great therapist and psychiatrist) helped pull me out of the depression. She reminded me of the importance of the small acts of self-care that we do every day.

I am often surprised how often I find myself overwhelmed with life and then I remember that I haven't eaten any food, drunk any water, or gotten 8 hours of sleep. Honestly, one of the best self-care measures is to ensure that our own basic physiological needs are met. This surprisingly simple solution (nutritious meals and snacks, proper hydration, and sleep) won't sell self-development or self-help merchandise, but it is the best first line of defense for feeling better.

When we give so much of our lives to others, it can be easy to skimp on the basics. So follow your mother's advice—eat an apple, drink a glass of water, and take a nap!

In all seriousness, when making your schedule and prioritizing your time, always put your basic needs first. Just like in the airplane, you have to put your oxygen mask on first before you help anyone else. You might need that early bedtime (for years, I have gone to bed at 8:30, because I just need that much sleep!), time to prepare lunches for the workday, or a pretty water bottle to encourage you to drink throughout the day.

This is advice that is so simple yet difficult to implement. I am the first one to stay up late, finishing a project or binging a TV show, skipping dinner because I was engrossed in grading papers, or remembering that I hadn't had a drop of water all day. I am also the first one to buy a new self-help book or try a new meditation app on my phone. We look for new and shiny ways to feel better, but sticking to the basics is so much more effective.

So, when you are feeling low, grumpy, or burned out, take a minute to reflect on your basic needs. How can you reprioritize your sleep, hydration, or nutrition to improve your mood, energy, or outlook?

The Next Level

If you are doing a reasonably good job of meeting your basic needs, then you can reflect on some higher needs. As important as our careers seem—we are changing the lives of students, after all—we also need to consider our whole selves.

Relationships

As humans, we have a need for relationships with others. As we move into adulthood and career focus, it is all too easy to let friendship, romantic partners, and family fall away. As teachers, we spend our working hours with little contact with other adults. Instead, our work companions are students who rely on us for educational and emotional support. Adult conversations happen, if we are lucky, during our 30-minute lunch breaks or at planning meetings during our free periods. Be kind to yourself, knowing that we also need friendships and relationship. It is okay to feed that part of yourself, whether that is happy hour with co-workers, a book club in your neighborhood, or activities at your community center or religious group. We all need time to socialize with others.

As an introvert, I am less likely to join a large group activity, but I also need to take the time to nurture individual friendships. Whether it is exchanging text messages with Jill or getting coffee with another mom from my child's school, these activities are vital to my well-being. These moments give me a chance to interact with an adult and fill my social needs, even as an introvert.

Similarly, it is all too easy as an educator to forget to prioritize our romantic relationships. If you are lucky enough to have found a life partner, it takes intentionality to put energy into fostering and caring for that relationship. Whether it is a weekly date night, sharing a cup of coffee in the morning, or a family dinner each night, intentionally carving out time to reconnect with your partner is an important part of caring for yourself. Your partner is your support system, and you will be more whole when you spend time with them and foster that connection.

Exercise and Nature

Another higher need that we all have is to keep our body moving and strong. This does not mean that we all need to hit the gym every day, run marathons, or lift our own body weight to be happy and enjoy life. However, neglecting our physical health will dampen our happiness. Even for the most unathletic among us (and trust me, I fit squarely into that box!), going outside, taking a walk, or generally moving your body can make a world of difference. Our bodies were made to move, and honoring their amazing capabilities is an excellent way to show kindness to ourselves.

Exercise is sometimes seen as a punishment. How many of us had a coach who made us run laps when we were late to practice? And if that is our outlook, it won't be a way for us to relax and take time for ourselves. So, a shift in mindset to one in which we can celebrate the ways in which our body moves can help us rethink our relationship with our bodies. Maybe it is stretching in a yoga class, or taking a weekend hike through a nearby nature trail, or dancing to your favorite song. These activities help us to appreciate ourselves and release some endorphins!

Along similar lines, being outside, breathing the fresh air, and feeling the sun on our skin have important effects on our mood. We, as humans, were also made to be in nature and part of our world. Spending time, even if only a few minutes, each day outside can help us recharge and connect back to our own selves. One of my favorite ways to reconnect with nature is to sit on my back porch during a rainstorm, hearing the patter of water hitting the roof, breathing in the fresh rain smells, and watching the streams form through the grass. This is truly restorative.

Mindfulness

Finally, as educators, we also tend to fill our thoughts with worry about others. Maybe it is concern for the students in our class, internal politics at school, curricular changes, pedagogical reflections, or even planning the next day's lessons. It can be difficult for us to "turn off" our thoughts. It can seem to us educators that our work is never done.

However, this state of anxiety is far from self-kindness and can lead to physical symptoms—insomnia, gastrointestinal distress, headaches, or worse (O'Connor et al., 2021). Worry, stress, and anxiety are not good for our physical or emotional health.

Used as a tool when worry gets to be too much or as a daily preventative practice, mindfulness can be an effective way to manage stress and be kind to yourself. Mindfulness can encompass anything from a few deep and intentional breaths, meditation, or a relaxing bath. Deep breathing, gratitude lists, grounding activities, and other simple activities can provide the calming space for you to reduce your anxiety and stress. In the Resources section, I have listed places where you can find more information about mindfulness.

Most of us have a special routine to relax—my personal favorite is a hot shower, a freshly made bed, and a good book. Maybe yours is in having a cup of tea, knitting, or gardening. Remember that these practices are vital to your own health and that prioritizing yourself means that you have the capacity to help others. Transformational kindness starts with self.

Therapy

Kindness to self is also knowing that you are important enough and deserving of help. If you or a friend had a hacking cough that persisted after drinking hot tea and taking cold medication, you would not hesitate to encourage them to see a doctor. On the same note, if taking care of your basic needs feels overwhelming, you have been feeling down for a while, simple mindfulness activities aren't helping your anxiety, or you just don't feel "right"—now is the time to seek help. You do not need to wait until you are absolutely miserable or facing a mental health crisis to seek out a therapist or counselor.

Many therapists will see you, even if only for a few sessions, to help you through a temporary difficult circumstance or to talk through a major life decision. Truth be told, most of us would benefit from a mental health check-in with a therapist on occasion.

Many employers offer an Employee Assistance Program (EAP) or similar service that provides short-term counseling at no cost. You can locate this information through the Human Resources Benefits office. It is also usually available to spouses and dependents. These appointments and calls are confidential and are not reported to your employer (unless, of course, you are in danger to yourself or others, in which case the mental health professional will contact the appropriate services to ensure your safety). If you need more mental health resources, please see the Resources section. I am not a mental health professional, and when life can feel overwhelming, please seek the help that you need. There are life circumstances that need more than a hot bath, deep breathing, a walk through nature, or a nap to overcome. Transformational kindness is reaching out for help.

Giving Grace

For a section on self-care, I have sure given you a lot of things to do! At the risk of sounding like a hypocrite, I know that for busy professionals it may be difficult (or even impossible) to practice the routines recommended in this chapter. (Seriously, in preparing this book for the publisher, I am definitely not getting the required 8 hours of sleep!)

This is the part of the book where I remind you that you can treat yourself with the same kindness that you would give to your best friend. Give yourself grace. In other words, forgive yourself for the mistakes you have made. Be kind to yourself.

You will not always be able to do it all. There are times when you won't meet your goals, and you will let people (or yourself) down. You will miss deadlines. You will forget to maintain relationships. You will sustain yourself on ice cream or peanut butter rather than actual meals. You will leave the laundry in a pile on the floor for longer than you would admit to your mother.

Before you berate yourself for not living up to your own expectations, consider how you would react to your best friend in the same circumstance. My guess is that you wouldn't tell them that they were failing or yell at them for not being better. No, you would give them a hug, reassure them about all the amazing things they have accomplished, and remind them of all of the wonderful things that they have to look forward to. So, try to speak to yourself like you would your best friend. That is being kind to yourself—giving yourself grace. Transformational kindness.

Words of Affirmation

Finally, dear reader, I have some words for you. When you are feeling down, read the following words from me to you:

> You are an amazing person, and there is no one on this planet that is you. You contribute to our world in ways that you will never know. Even when you can't be everything, you are something—and that something means the world to the lives that you touch every day. You are important, valuable, and special. Thank you for spreading your light to us each day.

Read this and then read it again. Read it over and over until you believe it—because it is the truth.

Because you have given your life and career to education and that is important work. There are plenty of clichés about teaching changing the world and our futures—but the reason they proliferate is because they speak to a truth about our society. Educators are essential—and you make a difference to our children, students, and communities. Even when we don't live up to our own expectations, our work is important, and we do change the world.

Afterword

I wrote this book in 2021 through 2022 as the COVID-19 pandemic continued to wear down on society, political and racial tensions in the US escalated, and our world felt more filled with divisiveness, violence, and hate. It is my sincere hope for this world that our schools and education systems can be part of the solution.

Transformational kindness towards our world can be taught, modeled, and shared. We have the power, collectively, to make our schools and classrooms places of safety, security, and love through the transformational power of kindness.

When our actions, speech, and policies are informed by a framework of kindness, we can change a generation of students. We, through true kindness, can help bring our communities to places that care about all of our members. This is not an easy task, or something that we can change overnight, but if we start practicing transformational kindness in our individual spheres of influence, it will spread. We will change the lives of our students, our communities, and eventually the world.

DOI: 10.4324/9781003250739-8

Resources

Kindness Overview

Deep Kindness: A Revolutionary Guide for the Way We Think, Talk, and Act in Kindness
By Houston Kraft (Simon Element, 2020)

Queen Bees and Wannabes: Helping Your Daughter Survive Cliques, Gossip, Boys, and the New Realities of Girl World
By Rosalind Wiseman (Harmony, 2016)

Radical Kindness: The Life-Changing Power of Giving and Receiving
By Angela C. Santomero (Harper Collins, 2019)

Help for Abuse Recovery

National Domestic Abuse Hotline
(800) 799-7233
Hours: 24 hours a day, 7 days a week
Text: START to 88788
https://www.thehotline.org/

DOI: 10.4324/9781003250739-9

The Emotional Abuse Recovery Workbook: Breaking the Cycle of Psychological Violence
By Theresa Comito (Rockridge Press, 2020)

Triumph Over Abuse: Healing, Recovery, and Purpose after an Abusive Relationship
By Christine E. Murray (Rutledge Press, 2021)

Toxic and Unhealthy Work Environments

Toxic Cultures at Work: The Eight Drivers of a Toxic Culture and a Process for Change
By James Cannon (Rutledge Press, 2022)

Working with You Is Killing Me: Freeing Yourself from Emotional Traps at Work
By Katherine Crowley and Kathi Elster (Business Plus, 2007)

Kindness in Leadership

Kindness in Leadership
Edited by Gay Haskins, Michael Thomas, & Lalit Johri (Routledge Press, 2018)

The Kind Leader
By Karyn Ross (Routledge Press, 2022)

Discrimination and Bias in Schools and Society

Implicit Bias in Schools: A Practitioner's Guide
By Gina Laura Gullo, Kelly Capatosto, & Cheryl Staats (Rutledge Press, 2019)

Pushout: The Criminalization of Black Girls in Schools
By Monique W. Morris (The New Press, 2016)

The New Jim Crow: Mass Incarceration in the Age of Colorblindness
By Michelle Alexander (The New Press, 2020)

When Black Students Excel: How Schools Can Engage and Empower Black Students
By Joseph F. Johnson, Jr., Cynthia L. Uline, & Stanley J. Munro (Rutledge Press, 2023)

School Security and Safety

Basic 40-Hour School Resource Officer Course Outline and Objectives
National Association of School Resource Officers (NASRO)
https://nasro.org/cms/wp-content/uploads/2014/04/NASRO-Basic-Course-Description-and-Outline.pdf

Policing the Schools: Strategies for Effective Principal–Police Partnerships
National School Safety and Security Services (NSSSS)
https://www.schoolsecurity.org/school-safety-and-communications-services/policing-the-schools-strategies-for-effective-principal-police-partnerships/

Position Statement on Police Involvement in Student Discipline
National Association of School Resource Officers (NASRO)
https://nasro.org/news/press-releases/nasro-position-statement-police-involvement-student-discipline/

Sociocultural Learning/Apprenticeship Models

Situated Learning: Legitimate Peripheral Participation
By Jean Lave & Etiénne Wegner (Cambridge University Press, 1991)

Classroom Management Resources

Hacking School Discipline: 9 Ways to Create a Culture of Empathy & Responsibility Using Restorative Justice
By Nathan Maynard & Brad Weinstein (Times 10 Publications, 2020)

Preventing Challenging Behavior in Your Classroom: Classroom Management and Positive Behavior Support
By Matt Tincani (Rutledge Press, 2022)

Teaching with Love and Logic: Taking Control of the Classroom
By Jim & Charles Fay (Love & Logic, 2016)

The High-Trust Classroom: Raising Achievement from the Inside Out
By Lonnie Moore (Rutledge Press, 2017)

Child Abuse and Neglect Resources

Child Welfare Information Gateway
Child Help USA
(800) 422-4453
List of State Reporting Sites:
https://www.childwelfare.gov/organizations/?CWIGFunction saction=rols:main.dspList&rolType=Custom&RS_ID=%205

National Domestic Abuse Hotline
(800) 799-7233
Hours: 24 hours a day, 7 days a week
Text: START to 88788
https://www.thehotline.org/

Prevent Child Abuse America
https://preventchildabuse.org/
https://www.healthyfamiliesamerica.org/

Trauma-Informed Practices for Early Childhood Educators: Relationship-Based Approaches that Support Healing and Build Relationship in Young Children
By Julie Nicholson, Linda Perez & Julie Kurtz (Rutledge Press, 2019)

Suicide and Self-Harm

Crisis Text Line
Text HOME to 741741
https://www.crisistextline.org/

National Alliance on Mental Illness
https://www.nami.org/Home
National Suicide Prevention Lifeline
(800)273-TALK (8255)
https://suicidepreventionlifeline.org/

Preventing Youth Suicide: Tips for Parents & Educators
National Association of School Psychologists
https://www.nasponline.org/resources-and-publications/resources-and-podcasts/school-safety-and-crisis/mental-health-resources/preventing-youth-suicide/preventing-youth-suicide-tips-for-parents-and-educators

Curricular Resources

A People's History of the United States
By Howard Zinn (Harper Perennial Modern Classics, 2015)

Educators for Social Justice
http://www.educatorsforsocialjustice.org/

Lies My Teacher Told Me: Everything Your American History Textbook Got Wrong
By James W. Loewen (The New Press, 2018)

Testing

The Truth about Testing: An Educator's Call to Action
By W. James Popham (ASCD, 2001)

Differentiation

How to Differentiate Instruction in Academically Diverse Classrooms
By Carol Ann Tomlinson (ASCD, 2017)

Teaching Gifted Kids in Today's Classroom: Strategies and Techniques Every Teacher Can Use
By Susan Winebrenner & Dina Brulles (Free Spirit Publishing, 2018)

Vertical Differentiation for Gifted, Advanced, and High-Potential Students
By Emily L. Mofield (Rutledge Press, 2022)

Universal Design for Learning

The UDL Guidelines
CAST organization
https://udlguidelines.cast.org/

Universal Design for Learning in the Early Childhood Classroom
By Pamela Brilliante & Karen Nemeth (Rutledge, 2022)

Response to Intervention (RTI) / Multi-Tiered System of Supports (MTSS)

Multi-tiered Systems of Support in Elementary Schools: The Definitive Guide to Effective Implementation and Quality Control
By Alison G. Clark & Katherine A. Dockweiler (Rutledge Press, 2020)

Reaching and Teaching Students Who Don't Qualify for Special Education: Strategies for the Inclusive Education For Diverse Learners
By Steven R. Shaw (Rutledge Press, 2022)

Rigor in the RTI and MTSS Classroom: Practice Tools and Strategies
By Barbara R. Blackburn & Bradley S. Witzel (Rutledge Press, 2018)

English Language Learners

Helping English Language Learners Meet the Common Core: Assessment and Instructional Strategies
By Paul Boyd-Batstone (Rutledge Press, 2013)

TESOL International Association
Teaching English to Speakers of Other Languages
https://www.tesol.org/

Gifted Students

Identifying and Serving Diverse Gifted Learners: Meeting the Needs of Special Populations in Gifted Education
By Jaime A. Castellano & Kimberly L. Chandler (Rutledge Press, 2022)

National Association for Gifted Children
https://www.nagc.org/

Teaching Gifted Children: Success Strategies for Teaching High-Ability Learners
By Jeff Danielian, C. Matthew Fugate, Elizabeth Fogarty (Rutledge Press, 2017)

Special and Exceptional Student Education

Council for Exceptional Children
https://exceptionalchildren.org/

Special Needs Advocacy Resource Book
By Rich Weinfeld & Michelle Davis (Rutledge Press, 2005)

The Complete Guide to Special Education: Expert Advice on Evaluations, IEPs, and Helping Kids in Schools
By Linda Wilmshurst & Alan W. Brue (Rutledge Press, 2018)

Culturally Responsive Teaching

Culturally Responsive Education in the Classroom: An Equity Framework for Pedagogy
By Adeyemi Stembridge (Rutledge Press, 2020)

Identity Affirming Classrooms: Spaces that Center Humanity
By Erica Buchanan-Rivera (Rutledge Press, 2022)

The Center for Culturally Responsive Teaching and Learning
https://www.culturallyresponsive.org/

LGBT Safe Spaces

Creating Safe and Supportive Learning Environments: A Guide for Working with Lesbian, Gay, Bisexual, Transgender, and Questioning Youth
Edited by Emily S. Fisher & Karen Komosa-Hawkins (Rutledge Press, 2013)

GLSEN
https://www.glsen.org/

GSA Network
https://gsanetwork.org/

Trevor Project
https://www.thetrevorproject.org/

Performance Assessment

Using Rubrics for Performance-Based Assessment: A Practical Guide to Evaluating Student Work
By Todd Stanley (Rutledge Press, 2019)

Inquiry Models of Teaching

Teaching Critical Thinking: Using Seminars for 21st Century Literacy
By Terry Roberts & Laura Billings (Rutledge Press, 2012)

The 5E's of Inquiry-Based Science
By Lakeena Chitman-Booker & Kathleen Kopp (Rutledge, 2013)

The Paideia Classroom: Teaching for Understanding
By Laura Billings & Terry Roberts (Rutledge Press, 1999)

Project-Based Learning

Creative Problem Solving: An Introduction
By Donald J. Treffinger, Scott G. Isaksen, & K. Brian Stead-Dorval (Rutledge Press, 2006)

Project-Based Learning for Gifted Students: A Step-By-Step Guide to PBL and Inquiry in the Classroom
By Todd Stanley (Rutledge Press, 2021)

Ready-to-Use Resources for Genius Hour in the Classroom: Taking Passion Projects to the Next Level
By Andi McNair (Rutledge Press, 2019)

Family and Parent Communications

Everyday Engagement: Making Students and Parents Your Partners in Learning
By Kay Ridnouer (ASCD, 2010)

Meet the Parents: How Schools Can Work Effectively with Families to Support Children's Learning
By Dorothy Lepkowska & Julie Nightingale (Rutledge Press, 2019)

Teaching Comprehensive Sexual Education

National Sexuality Education Standards
Sexual Information and Education Council of the United States (SIECUS)
https://siecus.org/resources/national-sexuality-education-standards-first-edition/

Tools for Teaching Comprehensive Human Sexuality Education: Lessons, Activities, and Teaching Strategies Utilizing the National Sexuality Education Standards
By Dominick Splendorio & Lori A. Reichel (Jossey-Bass, 2013)

Community Resources

Boy Scouts of America
https://www.scouting.org/

Girl Scouts of USA
https://www.girlscouts.org/

United Way Navigation Center for Community Resources
https://www.navigateresources.net/211communityresources/

YMCA
https://www.ymca.org/

Non-Partisan Election Resources

Fact Check.org
https://www.factcheck.org/

League of Women Voters
https://www.lwv.org/

Run for Office
https://www.runforoffice.org/

Teachers Unions

American Association of University Professors
https://www.aaup.org/

American Federation of Teachers
https://www.aft.org/

National Education Association
https://www.nea.org/

Self-Care

Everyday Self-Care for Educators: Tools and Strategies for Well-Being
By Carla Tantillo Philibert, Christopher Soto, & Lara Veon (Rutledge, 2020)

Mindfulness

Mindfulness in the Classroom: Mindful Principles for Social Emotional Learning
By Season Mussey (Rutledge, 2019)

One Minute Mindfulness Journal: 60-Second Self-Care Tools to Center Your Life
By Christopher Wells (Sourcebooks, 2020)

Walking the Teacher's Path with Mindfulness: Stories for Reflection and Action
By Richard Brady (Rutledge, 2021)

Therapy

Find a therapist
Psychology Today
https://www.psychologytoday.com/us/therapists

Search for Psychologist
American Psychological Association
https://locator.apa.org/

References

Acosta, R. (2010, November 17). Suspensions spark controversy after hunting firearms found in cars of Byron High School students. *Michigan Live*. https://www.mlive.com/news/flint/2010/11/suspensions_spark_controversy.html

Bolger, P. C., Kremser, J., & Walker, H. (2018). Detention or diversion? The influence of training and education on school police officer discretion. *Policing: An International Journal*, *42*(2), 255–269. doi: 10.1108/PIJPSM-01-2018-0007.

British Broadcasting Corporation (BBC). (2017, March 30). *School apologises for 'slut-shame' prom posters about appropriate dresses*. https://www.bbc.com/news/newsbeat-39444386

Centers for Disease Control and Prevention (CDC). (2019). *Youth risk behavior survey (YRBS)*. https://yrbs-explorer.services.cdc.gov/#/

Chamizo-Nieto, M. T., Arrivillaga, C., Rey, L., & Extremera, N. (2021). The role of emotional intelligence, the teacher-student relationship, and flourishing on academic performance in adolescents: a moderated mediation study. *Frontiers in Psychology*, *12*. doi:10.3389/fpsyg.2021.695067.

Chiu, A. (2019, September 24). Florida officer fired for 'traumatic' arrests of two 6-year-old students at school. *Washington Post*. https://www.washingtonpost.com/nation/2019/09/23/girl-tantrum-orlando-classroom-arrested-battery-school-investigation/

Cox, C. (2020, January 24). Texas teen banned by high school from attending graduation after refusing to cut dreadlocks. *USA Today*. https://www.usatoday.com/story/news/nation/2020/01/24/black-texas-teen-barred-high-school-after-graduation-not-cutting-dreadlocks/4562210002/

Curran, F. C. (2020). *The expanding presence of law enforcement in Florida schools*. University of Florida Education Policy Research Center. https://www.aclufl.org/sites/default/files/curran_-_the_expanding_presence_of_law_enforcement_in_florida_schools.pdf

Finkelhor, D. (2007). Prevention of sexual abuse through educational programs directed toward children. *Pediatrics-English Edition, 120*(3), 640–645. doi:10.1542/peds.2007-0754.

Gay, Lesbian, & Straight Education Network (GLSEN). (2019). *Mental health advocacy*. https://www.glsen.org/activity/mental-health-advocacy

Giano, Z., Williams, A. L., & Becnel, J. N. (2022). Grade retention and school dropout: comparing specific grade levels across childhood and early adolescence. *Journal of Early Adolescence, 42*(1), 33–57. doi:10.1177/02724316211010332.

Gomi, T. (2020). *Everyone poops*. New York: Chronicle Books.

Gurantz, O. (2021). How college credit in high school impacts postsecondary course-taking: The role of Advanced Placement exams. *Education Finance and Policy, 16*(2), 233–255. doi:10.1162/edfp_a_00298.

Heise, M., & Nance, J. P. (2021). "Defund the (school) police"? bringing data to key school-to-prison pipeline claims. *Journal of Criminal Law and Criminology, 111*(3), 717–772.

Heissel, J. A., Adam, E. K., Doleac, J. L., Figlio, D. N., & Meer, J. (2021). Testing, stress, and performance: How students respond physiologically to high-stakes testing. *Education Finance and Policy, 16*(2), 183–208. doi:10.1162/edfp_a_00306.

Högberg, B., & Horn, D. (2022). National high-stakes testing, gender, and school stress in Europe: A difference-in-differences analysis. *European Sociological Review, 2022*(1). 1–13. doi:10.1093/esr/jcac009.

Irwin, V., Zhang, J., Wang, X., Hein, S., Wang, K., Roberts, A., … & Purcell, S. (2021). *Report on the condition of education 2021*. NCES 2021-144. National Center for Education Statistics. https://files.eric.ed.gov/fulltext/ED612942.pdf

Jones, B. D. (2007). The unintended outcomes of high-stakes testing. *Journal of Applied School Psychology, 23*(2), 65–86. doi:https://doi.org/10.1300/J370v23n02_05.

Kim, J. (2018). School accountability and standard-based education reform: The recall of social efficiency movement and scientific management. *International Journal of Educational Development, 60*, 80–87. doi:10.1016/j.ijedudev.2017.11.003.

King, S., & Bracy, N. L. (2019). School security in the post-Columbine era: Trends, consequences, and future directions. *Journal of Contemporary Criminal Justice, 35*(3), 274–295. doi:10.1177/1043986219840188.

Klein, D. A., Ahmed, A. E., Murphy, M. A., Pearlman, A. T., Johnson, N., Gray, J. C., & Schvey, N. A. (2022). The mediating role of family acceptance and conflict on suicidality among sexual and gender minority youth. *Archives of Suicide Research, 2022*, 1–8. doi:10.1080/13811118.2022.2075815.

Leachman, M., & Figueroa, E. (2019, March 6). K-12 school funding up in most 2018 teacher-protest states, but still well below decade ago. *Center on Budget and Policy Priorities*, (p. 6).

Lenthang, M. (2021, March 27). 5-year-old boy allegedly detained, handcuffed and threatened by Maryland police. *ABC News*. https://abcnews.go.com/US/year-boy-allegedly-detained-handcuffed-threatened-maryland-police/story?id=76721492

Levenson, E., & Burnside, T. (2020, August, 11). Key West Police arrested an 8-year-old at school. His wrists were too small for the handcuffs. *CNN*. https://www.cnn.com/2020/08/11/us/8-year-old-boy-key-west-arrest-trnd/index.html

Loewen, J. W. (2008). *Lies my teacher told me: Everything your American history textbook got wrong*. New York: The New Press.

Marjory Stoneman Douglas High School Public Safety Act, Florida Statute § 7026. (2018).

Maslow, A. (1943). A theory of human motivation. *Psychological Review, 50*, 370–396.

Mowen, T. J., & Freng, A. (2019). Is more necessarily better? School security and perceptions of safety among students and parents in the United States. *American Journal of Criminal Justice, 44*(3), 376–394. doi:10.1007/s12103-018-9461-7.

National Association of School Psychologists (NASP). (2018). *Framework for safe and successful schools: Considerations and action steps* [Brief]. Bethesda, MD: National Association of School Psychologists. https://www.nasponline.org/schoolsafetyframework

National Center for Educational Statistics (NCES). (2022, March). *U.S. schools report increased teacher vacancies due to COVID-19 pandemic, new NCES data show*. https://nces.ed.gov/whatsnew/press_releases/3_3_2022.asp

National School Safety and Security Services (2019). Policing the schools: Strategies for effective principal – police partnerships. https://www.schoolsecurity.org/school-safety-and-communications-services/policing-the-schools-strategies-for-effective-principal-police-partnerships/

Novak, A. (2019). The school-to-prison pipeline: An examination of the association between suspension and justice system involvement. *Criminal Justice and Behavior*, *46*(8), 1165–1180. doi:10.1177/0093854819846917.

O'Connor, D. B., Thayer, J. F., & Vedhara, K. (2021). Stress and health: A review of psychobiological processes. *Annual Review of Psychology*, *72*(1), 663–688. doi:https://doi.org/10.1146/annurev-psych-062520-122331.

Popham, W. J. (2001). Teaching to the test?. *Educational Leadership*, *58*(6), 16–21.

Rabbitte, M., & Enriquez, M. (2019). The role of policy on sexual health education in schools. *The Journal of School Nursing*, *35*(1), 27–38. doi:https://doi.org/10.1177/1059840518789240.

Riddle, T., & Sinclair, S. (2019). Racial disparities in school-based disciplinary actions are associated with county-level rates of racial bias. *Proceedings of the National Academy of Sciences*, *116*(17), 8255–8260. doi:10.1073/pnas.1808307116.

Robinson, C. (2022, May 31). Arrest report: Florida 10-year-old texted picture of AR-15 rifles, said 'get ready'. *Associated Press*. https://www.wesh.com/article/florida-child-school-shooting-threat/40150970#

Rogers, C. R. (1957). The necessary and sufficient of therapeutic personality change. *Journal of Consulting Psychology*, *21*(2), 95–103. doi:10.1037/h0045357.

Rogoff, B., Turkanis, C. G., & Bartlett, L. (2001). *Learning together: Children and adults in a school community*. New York: Oxford University Press.

Shields, L. (2021, April 12). Public records show more dress code violations for female students in St. Johns County schools. *First Coast News*. https://www.firstcoastnews.com/article/entertainment/television/programs/gmj/public-records-disproportionate-dress-code-violations-female-students-st-johns-county-schools/77-a2bd2163-f28d-427b-9815-7e9b8b5c8cd1

Sobol, E. (2022, May 31). Middle school student arrested for making school threats in Old Saybrook. *Eyewitness News* 3. https://www.wfsb.com/2022/05/31/middle-school-student-arrested-making-school-threats-old-saybrook/

Steiner, E. D., & Woo, A. (2021). *Job-related stress threatens the teacher supply: Key findings from the 2021 State of the U.S. Teacher Survey.*

Santa Monica, CA: RAND Corporation, 2021. https://www.rand.org/pubs/research_reports/RRA1108-1.html

Stubbs, R. (2019, April 17). A wrestler was forced to cut his dreadlocks before a match. His town is still looking for answers. *Washington Post*. https://www.washingtonpost.com/sports/2019/04/17/wrestler-was-forced-cut-his-dreadlocks-before-match-his-town-is-still-looking-answers/

Taliaferro, L. A., & Muehlenkamp, J. J. (2017). Nonsuicidal self-injury and suicidality among sexual minority youth: Risk factors and protective connectedness factors. *Academic Pediatrics*, *17*(7), 715–722. doi:10.1016/j.acap.2016.11.002.

Tomaszewski, J. (2011). Unbelievable school decisions: Kids don prison jumpsuits. *Education World*. https://www.educationworld.com/a_admin/archives/unbelievable_school_decisions/prison_jumpsuits.shtml

Tomlinson, C. A. (2001). *How to differentiate instruction in mixed-ability classrooms*. Alexandria, VA: ASCD.

Walton, A. G. (2012, April 24). Why Autistic children are bullied more – And bully in return. *Forbes*. https://www.forbes.com/sites/alicegwalton/2012/04/24/why-autistic-children-are-bullied-more/?sh=78c3eb8e408c

Whitehead, R., Pringle, J., Scott, E., Milne, D., & McAteer, J. (2019). *The relationship between a trusted adult and adolescent health and education outcomes*. National Health Services Scotland. https://dera.ioe.ac.uk/34105/1/the-relationship-between-a-trusted-adult-and-adolescent-health-outcomes_6588.pdf

Wiseman, R. (2016). *Queen bees and wannabes: Helping your daughter survive cliques, gossip, boys, and the new realities of girl world*. New York: Harmony.

Woods, M., & Carr, B. (2022, March 16). Kindergarten student brings Jose Cuervo mix to class in Livonia, shared it with 4 others: School officials say disciplinary measures will be taken. *Click on Detroit*. https://www.clickondetroit.com/news/local/2022/04/16/elementary-school-student-brings-alcohol-to-class-in-livonia-later-shares-drink-with-four-students/